Alamo Doughboy
Marching into the Heart
of Kaiser's Germany during World War I

Jennifer Rude Klett

Branden Books, Boston

Reprinted material from *Five Days In October*: *The Lost Battalion Of World War I* by Robert H. Ferrell, by permission of the University of Missouri-Press. Copyright © 2005 by the Curators of the University of Missouri.

Library of Congress Cataloging-in-Publication Data
Klett, Jennifer Rude.
  Alamo doughboy : marching into the heart of Kaiser's Germany during World War I / Jennifer Rude Klett.
      pages cm
  Includes bibliographical references and index.
  ISBN 978-0-8283-2507-3 (pbk. : alk. paper) -- ISBN 978-0-8283-2508-0 (e-book)
1. Knott, George, 1896-1977.
2. Soldiers--United States--Biography.
3. United States. Army. Infantry Division, 90th--Biography.
4. United States. Army. American Expeditionary Forces—
      Biography.
5. World War, 1914-1918--Campaigns--France.
6. Raymond (Minn.)--Biography.
I. Title.

    D570.390th .K55 2014
    940.4'1273092aB--dc23
                    2013044141

Paperback ISBN 9780828325073
E-Book ISBN 9780828325080
Branden Books
PO Box 812094
Wellesley MA 02482
www.brandenbooks.com

To the nine million
Who never made it home.

"Was anybody shooting at you?"
-George "Judge" Knott
(responding to his son-in-law after hearing complaints about the
army in 1963)

"No."
-Son-in-law

"Well then, you had a pretty good day."
-Judge

CONTENTS

Preface

The First World War dramatically altered nearly everything in the world, yet we as Americans know next to nothing about it. Hopefully, this book will help change that.

This true story follows the path of a young man named Judge Knott, his two brothers and two cousins, all of whom grew up in the same small town in Minnesota. This detailed account of their experiences in the war is told through family interviews, US Army regiment and division histories, service records, newspaper accounts, and letters from *over there*. I found it simply amazing to be able to pinpoint one man's steps in the chaos of war nearly one hundred years later by the week, day and even the hour, when writing this book, especially since Judge's federal service record was a casualty of the infamous 1973 fire at the National Personnel Records Center in Missouri.

I found his story fascinating.

There has been comparatively little written about the United States in World War I, especially from the perspective of a neglected private in the trenches. Just traveling overseas was a monumental adventure for most at that time.

What did going over the top mean to infantrymen? What was it like being a runner? What about influenza and disease? Trench warfare? Aviation combat? Chemical warfare? Who were the Texas Brigade? Who were the Lost Battalion? What happened on November 11, 1918? How did the war affect the entire family? The hometowns? How did soldiers cope once back home if they were lucky enough to survive the brutal physical and emotional trauma of war?

The historical significance of the First World War cannot be overstated. It reshaped the entire twentieth century. Its ramifications are still being felt. The rise of communism and its subsequent regimes and wars (Korea, Vietnam); World War II (some historians consider it a continuation of World War I) and its holocaust (the first modern day genocide inflicted on the Armenians occurred in the First World War with the world casting a blind eye to it); the Cold War; and Middle East conflicts . . . all have roots in the Great War.

It's been nearly one hundred years since the war began. Today, the indescribable carnage, historical importance, and modern-day consequences of World War I are sadly glossed over in school classrooms and virtually ignored by media. American public libraries can easily have ten times the books about World War II over World War I on the nonfiction history shelves. And that doesn't even include biographies, movies, documentaries, etc.

How can we begin to understand current ethnic, religious, and geo-political conflicts without possessing knowledge about the years 1914 to 1918? We still commemorate Veterans Day, but what do we know about its predecessor Armistice Day?

We've all seen the iconic twentieth-century war memorials in Washington DC, possibly experiencing them in person. World War II, Korean War, Vietnam War. They help us reflect, learn, and honor the sacrifices. Do you remember the national World War I memorial? No, because it doesn't exist. It has been disregarded in this country, along with much of the war itself. Fortunately, steps are underway to correct that shameful absence (please visit www.wwimemorial.org).

The stories of the First World War must not be forgotten. For many years, George "Judge" Knott was just my grandfather. No real story there, or so I thought. Then in 2005, an aunt gave me his war letters, lovingly cherished and handed down from her aunts. Suddenly, my grandfather was not just an old man anymore.

We've met the so-called greatest generation, now let's meet the generation that raised them. I invite you to look up your own grandfather or great-grandfather. It's as easy as going to your local library, which may have free online genealogical databases. You may be surprised. While they may not call attention to themselves, the quiet accounts of history may still be present.

The doughboys are all gone now. There can be no honor flights. It's too late to thank them. But, we can remember them.

The Great War changed Judge's life, and it changed the world. Read on and meet Judge the doughboy. He was there and this is his story.

Jennifer Rude Klett
2013

The surging sea of human life forever onward rolls,
And bears to the eternal shore its daily freight of souls;
Though bravely sails our bark today, pale Death sits at the prow,
And few shall know we ever lived a hundred years from now.

A Hundred Years From Now, poem by Mary A. Ford

1 – It's A Long Way To Minnesota

On Halloween night 1918, Judge Knott tried to rest knowing it was coming again, and it would be his duty to confront it head-on. The gripping horror, the explosions, the machine gun bullets, the wounded and the grotesque corpses that lay where they fell. The ugliest reality of life. At pre-dawn, the time when lightness wrestles with the darkness and the outcome is still unclear, the US shelling began.

Private Knott held up about two and a half miles west of the Meuse River near Verdun, France, waiting for the infantry to takes its turn at a full-frontal assault. His battalion had successfully relieved one that was spent, without incident of friendly fire, which was always a risk in the forward zone. He was in just about the last place on earth he ever expected to be in the middle of a world calamity doing something unfathomable. He was 4,000 miles from his home state of Minnesota preparing to attack in the largest US Army battle ever waged. It was unprecedented. Dreaded Verdun had been the site of indescribable carnage for the French. Like an unwelcome ghost of the past, a heavy shadow of death, failure, and doom had fallen over Judge.

Judge would soon suffer the warmest reception he would ever encounter. Nothing in his short life had prepared him for the call from Uncle Sam, except prayer. Judge was a praying man and he was doing a lot of praying lately. Praying for his two brothers and two cousins who were also part of the enormous wave of khaki-olive clad Americans who came to help end the death and

destruction of the past four years. The Knott boys found themselves part of the American Expeditionary Forces, a large American army fighting overseas, which was also unprecedented. Just
where were his brothers Ten and Bill? His cousins, Ray and
Carlton? Were they still alive?

Judge prayed he would make it home. The problem was, he
figured the Huns would be praying the same thing. Whose prayers
would be answered? Who would die and who would live? If only
he had a guardian angel.

*Almighty God: Please give me courage and strength. Please
protect me and my brothers. Please get me home again . . .*

H-hour was coming before the darkness would vanish, and
Judge with the Texas boys were to lead the attack into no man's
land. He was confident his battalion of Tough 'Ombres, although
weakened in size, was ready to deliver. But he also knew that in
just a few hours, the boys would be falling on all sides of him, torn
to pieces. More of his company's men would die in the next few
days than at any other time.

This would be Judge's deadliest fight in the war and he was
doing his best to prepare. He had to brace himself. He had to keep
going. If the only way home was to go forward, then Judge would
go over the top. He had to kill or be killed. It was that simple and it
was that hard. The Germans would bitterly and skillfully defend
the territory they had mastered in over four years of occupation.
They were exceptionally prepared.

The doughboys who survived the next few hours and days
would never forget what happened. Some would never speak of it
again. The first worldwide war would become personal, even
define some. These were young men whose destinies were still a
mysterious blank slate, except for the deep impression the war
would inevitably leave. They would carry the haunting and
intimate memories that would color their world for the rest of their
days.

The lice were back, so were the rats, the trenches, the mud, the funk holes, the barbed wire, the shell holes, the ruins, the tree stumps, the pock-marked barren gray landscape. It was near freezing, getting bitterly cold as the war went on, and the doughboys were insufficiently supplied. There were just not enough overcoats, blankets, food, and drinkable water.

Judge could talk tough, a typical trait of many young men. The truth was, he desperately wanted to see his mother again. And, then there was Duke. Wasn't it just last Halloween that he was tipping over outhouses back home in Minnesota? How in the world did his life come to this?

Judge with Duke c. 1915; family photo.

What victory can cheer a mother's heart,
When she looks at her blighted home?
What victory can bring her back
All she cared to call her own?
Let each mother answer
In the years to be,
Remember that my boy belongs to me!

I Didn't Raise My Boy To Be A Soldier, 1915 song by Alfred
Bryan

2 - The Knott Boys

George "Judge" Robert Knott was about as amiable a man you
could care to know. A tall man with curly red hair, he found the
humor in just about any situation. One of nine children, he was
known as the family clown, someone who loved sports and telling
stories. He was the family's second George, as an earlier son
named George died in infancy.

Born of humble beginnings in 1896 in Raymond, Minnesota to
Dutch immigrant parents, George was nicknamed Judge because
his father, William Knott, was the town's justice of the peace at the
time he was born.

During Judge's childhood, the village of Raymond consisted of
a couple hundred people set amid mostly Scandinavian, Dutch and
German immigrant farmsteads in rural Minnesota. The downtown
consisted of a mere two blocks, running along the railroad tracks--
its ties to the outside world.

Like many rural communities, there was a symbiotic relationship between the downtown businesses and the area farmers, as
both needed the other to prosper. The most prominent downtown
structure was the McKinley building at Spicer Avenue and Cofield

Street. The McKinley building housed the bank, and a local meat market known for its homemade ring bologna.

In the Knott home located about three blocks from downtown, Judge shared a bedroom with his three brothers. Tennus or Ten (also known as Hank) was the oldest born in 1893, then Bill born in 1894, Judge came next, followed by Roy (also known as Punk) born in 1899. Ten and Bill shared a bed; Judge and Roy shared another.

Judge had five sisters, all of whom shared a bedroom. The oldest was Emma, followed by Effie, Etta, Grace, and Jeanette. Judge was close to Etta, who was five years older. Not surprisingly, Etta was also known for her sense of humor. She was a bright girl who became one of four high school graduates of the first 1911 class at Raymond's school. Later, she became a teacher.

Red hair ran in the Knott family. Of the boys, Judge and Ten had red hair. Sisters Emma and Effie were also redheads.

The terrain surrounding the somewhat isolated village of Raymond was extremely flat and ideal for farming. It was a typical Midwestern town, nothing out of the ordinary. There was an ongoing debate over who was more stubborn, the Germans or the Norwegians. The Germans would accuse the Norwegians of being the more stubborn, the Norwegians visa versa. The Germans were more competitive, so they usually ended up winning that argument. Raymond's population seemed a somewhat homogenous bunch. However, Sundays told a different story.

On Sunday mornings in Raymond churches, the ethnic traditions ran deep. Most of the Germans went to the Lutheran church, the Norwegians went to a different Lutheran church, and the Dutch attended the Dutch Reformed church. Many churches held services in their parishioners' native language. The latecomers were the Catholics, who were looked upon with suspicion by many of the established town folk. The churches were central to community life.

Some of the maverick Christians, including the Knott family, attended the Methodist Episcopal Church in Raymond. The family was historically Dutch Reformed, but Judge's uncle Henry G. Knott began the new church in 1890. The family followed and became Methodists, evidently they were more loyal to blood ties than denominational customs.

For Judge, his faith became a foundation that would help him endure the coming chaos of the world.

Tall and lanky, Judge Knott was a distinctive looking young man. His warm-toned freckled skin, fair facial hair, and curly red "mane" gave him a monochromatic tawny hue, with the exception of his blue eyes. He sort of resembled actor Bert Lahr's portrayal of the lion in the 1939 movie *The Wizard of Oz*.

Judge was predominantly known for his sense of humor. Frequently, his siblings were the unappreciative victims of his practical jokes.[1]

One evening, Etta was waiting for a gentlemen caller. Judge put on a disguise, snuck out, and knocked on the door. An elated Etta ran to open the door, and was quickly grabbed and kissed. Imagine her surprise when she found it wasn't her suitor but her little brother.

Judge and his brother Bill were known to tie his sisters to the clothesline with their hair braids. Frequently, Judge's comical lines erupted after bedtime, which made everyone laugh. Someone would wonder aloud who was on the pot in the dark (the home had no indoor facilities). George would reply something silly like, "It must be a skunk."

Sometimes, Judge received his comeuppance.

According to family lore, one incident involved sugar. Sugar was a luxury that Judge and the others were forbidden to person-ally raid. Once, he snuck some on his bread and slipped outside, only to meet his older brothers Ten and Bill, the enforcers. When asked what was on his bread, Judge cagily replied, "salt," and quickly crammed the bread in his mouth. Naturally suspicious, the two brothers got Judge down, sat on him and tasted what was left on the side of his mouth. Then, they gave him a whipping. Bossy and lively, Bill had a reputation for being a good fighter, unfortunately for Judge. And, as tall as Judge was, his older brothers were just as tall if not taller.

The Knott family had rules. Before they ate meals, everyone had to be at the table ready to give thanks. Then, his father would pray for several long minutes in Dutch. Sometimes unable to restrain himself from sneaking peaks at his father's long beard wiggling during the prayer, Judge would giggle, and would be sent from the table.

Judge's father William Knott operated a small cream, egg, and poultry business in Raymond. He was a strict authoritarian.

According to Judge's oldest daughter, Mildred Knott Robbins, who formally interviewed Judge during the 1970s, William Knott pulled Judge out of school after the eighth grade and had him work as a farmhand.[2] Ten had also left school after the eighth grade; and of the four brothers, only Bill attended high school, completing three years but not graduating.

"The farm was several miles out in the country. He walked there, worked eight hours, and walked home. He was paid twenty-five cents a day. His dad kept all of the money. Judge said that he was so tired he could hardly put one foot in front of the other. But when he got home, his mother would hug and kiss him and tell him what a good son he was. He felt eight feet tall. Sometimes she would give him back five cents to spend on himself," Mildred said.

Strikingly dissimilar from his father, Judge's mother was said to be a tenderhearted, charitable woman, and Judge took after her. Judge was a merciful man who sympathized with those less well off. In those days, hobos drifted into town. Judge would pilfer his family's vegetables and eggs and sneak off to a nearby lake where the hobos congregated. They would make soup and fry eggs together, sharing both a meal and fellowship.[3]

Despite tough economic conditions for many, those living in Raymond enjoyed a time of peaceful and remote simplicity.

In Europe, it was an absurdly different story. It was a period of complete shambles and instability, with the Great War beginning in 1914, and the Russian revolution erupting in 1917. On April 6, 1917, the US Congress declared war against the Central powers of Austria-Hungary, Germany, Bulgaria and the Ottoman Empire (Turkey). A violent transformation for much of the world was underway and the untested United States was about to enter the global arena.

This meant things were about to seriously change for the Knott family. A local draft board was formed in nearby Kandiyohi County seat Willmar on May 17, 1917. Annie Knott had four draft-age sons--a mother's nightmare during wartime. She would soon see three of her four sons go off to war.

Judge's brother Bill was the first brother to be drafted. Judge was next, followed by Ten. Bill left Willmar September 22 of 1917 to join the Eighty-eighth Division, and later became part of the Eighty-second "All American" Division with the 307th Engineers. He initially reported to Camp Dodge, Iowa, the closest camp to Raymond, Minnesota.

Ten, the last of the Knott brothers to go, did not leave until the following spring. He left May 3, 1918 for Camp Wadsworth, South Carolina as part of the Sixth Division.

Roy, the youngest son at age 18, was not initially drafted as the first registration affected men ages 21 to 31 years. Later, it would be expanded to ages 18 to 45. Roy was eager to join his brothers.

Judge had two cousins, Ray and Carlton Knott, who also served in the war. Ray and Carlton were the sons of Henry Knott who started the Methodist church in Raymond. The Knott relations were close, spending most Sundays and holidays together.

Ray and Carlton Knott spent most of their childhood in Raymond, but both brothers had moved out of state before entering the war. At age 18, Ray left Minnesota after two years of high school to teach in North Dakota. In the spring of 1914, he visited Minnesota and returned to North Dakota with his brother Carlton, who also sought to strike out on his own at age 20.

Both brothers ended up in Great Falls, Montana. Ray became a stenographer; Carlton was a chauffeur.

On June 5, 1917, the very first day to register for the war, Ray and Carlton registered from Great Falls, Montana. Ray enlisted two months later at Fort George Wright in Spokane, Washington; Carlton was later inducted.

Twenty-six-year-old Ray joined the Aero Squadron. He was first assigned to Kelly Field, San Antonio, Texas. Then, he went to Long Island, New York as a headquarter secretary to General Mason M. Patrick.[4]

Carlton, at age 24, was inducted from Coeur d'Alene, Idaho, but not until June 27, 1918. His 1917 draft registration stated he was married with one dependent child. "Dependent family" was cited as reason for exemption from the draft. The registrar also listed "broken arches" as a disability.

Soon, however, the situation changed for Carlton. By the next summer, he became the last Knott boy to join the war effort. According to his military record, he was listed as divorced by July of 1918 with no mention of a dependent child. His residence was now Coeur d'Alene, Idaho. Once inducted from Idaho, Carlton was sent to Camp Lewis, Washington assigned to the 166 Depot Brigade. Later, he was transferred to the 158th Infantry, Fortieth "Sunshine" Division at Camp Kearney, California.

As for Carlton's flat feet, while noted on his Report of Physical Examination of March 1918, they couldn't have been too dysfunctional because he was soon assigned to the infantry of all things.

Ray and Carlton's father Henry was an interesting character. Immigrating from Holland in 1871 with friends and relatives, he originally settled near Chicago, Illinois. Henry became influenced by the famous Christian evangelist Dwight L. Moody and became a lay preacher in the Chicago slums.[5] He married a German woman named Bertha D. Kraatz.

Henry, and much of the Knott clan, relocated to Roseland, Minnesota in 1886; soon after they came to nearby Raymond. In 1890, the dedicated and faithful Henry organized a Methodist church in Raymond, and served the congregation without salary for a number of years. After Henry died in 1900, Bertha remarried John Phiefer, a widower with children, and continued living in Raymond.

Judge was drafted September 8, 1917 by the local board of Kandiyohi County. Judge was 21 years old, about 6 ft. 2 in. tall. He lived at home, working as a farmhand for a Dutch family friend named Ben Mielker. Judge had a beloved dog named Duke who accompanied him everywhere, even herding cows. Duke, his faithful friend, was a black and white fox terrier – reportedly a good hunter.

Judge received his Notice of Call, and on September 14 at 8:00 a.m., he reported to Willmar for a physical examination.

The Willmar Republican Gazette ran a big spread in their newspaper on the departing recruits (although it appeared on December 26, 1918 after the war ended . . . so much for the profession of journalism back then or maybe they were running sort of a recap?). "Thirty young men who left Saturday, April 27, 1918," it read below their photograph. In the middle of the photograph, Judge literally stood out as he was about a head taller than most of the men and held the American flag.

The average US recruit was 21 to 23 years old, about 5 ft. 7 in. tall, and weighed 142 pounds.[6] Seven out of ten were draftees. Thirty-one percent were illiterate and eighteen percent were foreign born.

Minnesota was one of the states that provided healthier, stockier recruits as about seventy to eighty percent passed their physicals.[7] Rural boys like Judge were found healthier than urban boys. With its Nordic immigrants, Minnesota provided the tallest recruits from the northern states.[8] All the Knott boys were listed as tall with blue eyes on their registration forms, except Ray who was listed as medium height.

Soon, the time came for Judge to leave the haven of his childhood hometown and close ties of family and community.

Judge said his goodbyes to loved ones, neighbors, and sweetheart Ruby Wagner, and walked downtown Raymond to catch the train to Willmar on April 26, 1918. His dog Duke walked with him. Once on the bank corner, Judge sternly looked at Duke, told him to "stay", crossed the road and got on the train.

By the time Judge left to join the army and report to Camp Dodge, Iowa, he had turned 22. He had led an unaffected, simple life. According to relatives, he had never left small-town Raymond until age 18. But, his country had called him and he would answer.

Judge's world had been a striking contrast to the world at large. Germany and its allies were at war with the United States, Canada, Brazil, Russia, Japan, India, Nepal, New Zealand, Australia, South Africa, and much of Europe.

Little did Judge know that he would soon play a part in a tragedy of such immense proportion that it would entirely reshape the course of world history. The horrible carnage, destruction, and suffering of the war were already a reality for millions of people. The world was rapidly changing, and Judge was about to change with it. The powerful experience of war would, no doubt, affect him the rest of his life.

Judge was about to become a doughboy.

The Knott Boys In World War I.
Top: Judge; Middle (l-r): Ten, Bill;
Bottom (l-r): Carton, Ray. Photos
from the *Kandiyohi County In the
World War, 1917-1919*; and 360th
Infantry history book.

(l-r): Judge Knott with dog Duke; siblings Bill, Etta, Ten,
Jean, Grace, Effie, Roy c. 1916 at the Knott home; family photo.

Judge Knott holding the flag, leaving Willmar, Minnesota on April 26, 1918; photo from the *Willmar Republican Gazette.*

Our country's in it, men,
Just like the "Minute" Men,
We're going to forge our way to victory,
To save Democracy,
We've got to conquer Germany.

Our Country's In It Now, We've Got To Win It Now 1918
song by Arthur Buy Empeys

3 – The Alamo's "Hell Fire And A Fuzzy-O"

Initially, Judge reported to Camp Dodge in Johnston, Iowa as part of the Eighty-eighth Division, 352nd Infantry Regiment, Company F. It was the same camp his brother Bill first reported to months previous, but Bill had transferred out of the division by January 1918, so there would be no brother reunion.

The first of many war letters to be read, and answered, began arriving at the Knott home in the fall of 1917, after Bill was sent to Camp Dodge, where he spent his first few months in the army. In an October 18 letter, he wrote about receiving a suitcase of goodies, including candy.

Then in January 1918, he is transferred to the Eighty-second "All-American" Division, 307th Engineers, Company C in Camp Gordon, Georgia where he helped fellow recruits read and write. In spring, he is sent to Camp Mills, Long Island, New York to await his departure from the United States. One week before he is set to leave in May, he jokes about soon meeting French girls. "I may find a real girl in France. How would you like that? Have a French sister in law," he wrote.

On May 14, 1918 he sent a letter to his mother, Annie.

Dearest mother and rest:

*That sure was some letter from Judge. Will have to write
him. Maybe he can stay in Dodge for that is a good camp
besides the last two I was in and he aught to make good if
he wants two. I was crazy to leave but a man don't know
when he has it good. Wants to fight but I ain't any better
than the rest so hear goes. . .*
Bill

A few days later, Bill wrote again.

Dear sister and rest:
*Will send you my address as it will be from now on till I get
back to U.S.A. Am well and feeling good and crazy to see
how much of a man I am . . . wish I could of gone home for
a few days. . . good bye till you hear from me again.*
Bill

For Judge, fate intervened, and he was transferred out of Camp
Dodge within days.

For the first time in his life, Judge left the Midwest. He would
soon become an honorary Texan. Reassigned to fill the ranks of
the Ninetieth Division at Camp Travis in San Antonio, Judge the
Minnesotan was destined to live and fight with the Texas boys for
the remainder of the war.

Camp Travis was just north of Kelly Field, where Judge's
cousin Ray was first assigned. But, Ray had long-since transferred
so there would be no cousin reunion, either. While Texas had three
National Guard camps, Camp Travis was the only National Army
camp for a draftee division in the state.

Texas supplied a large number of men in the war, over 161,000
men. Only the states of New York, Pennsylvania, Illinois, and
Ohio exceeded this number.[1]

Along with Minnesota and other Midwestern states, the states of
Texas and Oklahoma (which mainly comprised the Ninetieth

Division) produced a higher percentage of fit draftees, between seventy and eighty percent passed their physicals.[2] The robust Texans also had the distinction of being the tallest recruits in the nation by nearly an inch.[3]

Many Texans and Oklahomans made their living on rural ranches, possessing valuable experience with using wire cutters, something that would soon come in handy with the "devil's rope" barbed wire defenses strung all over parts of France.

In Texas, the Ninetieth Division had been depleted in the spring of 1918 to replenish other divisions. Judge became part of the last shipment of about 5,000 replacements to join the division before it departed for overseas. Recruits filled the ranks of the Ninetieth back to nearly full strength by May, the largest group coming from Camp Dodge with men from Minnesota, Iowa, Illinois, and the Dakotas.

Camp Travis, built in 1917 as one of sixteen National Army Camps erected for the war, was located on the northeastern outskirts of the city of San Antonio.[4] It abutted Fort Sam Houston and included all of old Camp Wilson, a National Guard camp along with a huge parcel of sandy land. Camp Travis was named for Texas hero William B. Travis, a defender of the Alamo. Camp Travis only existed for a few years; it was absorbed by Fort Sam Houston in 1922.

Originally, the Ninetieth Division consisted of Texans and Oklahomans, which seemed fitting as the Republic of Texas had embraced a large part of territory, part of which became the state of Oklahoma. Many of its settlers were from Texas. "Together, they represented the spirit, the aggressiveness, the manhood of the great Southwest," wrote Major George Wythe, the official division historian, in *A History of the 90th Division*, in 1920.

The division was divided into two brigades. The 179th was designated as the Oklahoma Brigade. The 180th Brigade came to be known as the Texas Brigade, which Judge was assigned to. Judge fit right in with the tall Texans. With replacement recruits, nearly every state in the union was eventually represented in the Ninetieth Division.

Judge was assigned to the 360th Infantry Regiment, Company G. By May, the 360th would be back up to its maximum strength of 3721 men. Even within the 180th Texas Brigade, the 360th Regiment was considered the more Texan regiment (over the 359th) with draftees primarily coming from southern and eastern Texas. It had a reputation of being a singing regiment.[5] The 360th regimental yell was:

The bear jumped over the panther bluff, hell fire and a fuzzy-O![6]

A live brown bear mascot of the 360th, reportedly named Sable, also attracted attention within the division. In his book, *The 90th Division In World War I*, author historian Lonnie J. White mentions a "pet" bear named Teddy who had been brought to camp by several University of Texas draftees in the fall of 1917. The 360th had won custody of Teddy, or Sable as he became to be known, in an athletic competition in November.[7] A connection between Sable and the bear in the regimental yell is possible, but the exact meaning or origin of the 360th yell has been elusive.

The division was commonly known as the Alamo division and adopted a patch of a red T and O for Texas and Oklahoma. Just before the armistice, each division in the AEF was ordered to submit a design for an insignia to be worn on the upper left arm. The Alamo nickname, however, did not represent the Oklahomans, so it was not included in the patch. The press still often referred to the division as Alamo. Other nicknames included Tough 'Ombres, Rattlesnake, Outlaw, and Tear On division.

By the end of April 1918, the last Camp Dodge replacements had arrived.

The train stopped right in Camp Travis, and new recruits were immediately examined for contagious diseases. In the preceding fall and winter, Camp Travis experienced outbreaks of measles, pneumonia, meningitis, flu and mumps with some men dying. In February, over ten percent of the 28,416 men were ill with 1,782 undergoing hospital treatment and 1,035 hospitalized.[9] The Ninetieth Division needed all the healthy recruits it could get in order to be combat ready.

Valuables were then sealed in a large envelope. Later, recruits stripped naked, showered and underwent thorough examinations single file by doctor after doctor. Civilian clothes were mailed home. Fingerprints were taken, scars documented (Judge had four noted), and new clothes were distributed. Pedigrees were recorded and more clothes and blankets were handed out. The men were inoculated in both arms against smallpox and typhoid, marched out, and went into their barracks. The "ruddy" complexioned Judge weighed in at 152 pounds and needed a size 10E pair of boots.

Once again, the division began the laborious training of green recruits, working day and night, even Saturdays, and Sunday afternoons. Men spent fifteen hours a day at the rifle range. Judge earned an aggregate score of 147 on his slow and rapid fire rifle practice at distances ranging from 100 to 650 yards.[10]

All forms of athletics and sports were encouraged at Camp Travis including baseball, football, wrestling, basketball, tug-of-war, and track. This mostly likely would have appealed to Judge, who loved sports. However, he arrived with the last large group of replacements and they probably did not have the luxury of time nor the energy for diversions such as athletics. Half holidays on Wednesday and Saturday evening were abandoned.

Training was also held on Sundays after the 360th conducted outdoor church service, weather permitting, with the entire regiment attending.[11] Judge, a Methodist, was one of the second-largest religious denomination within the division at 6,144 men (behind the Baptists). Out of the 28,000 men, nearly all were listed as Christian, a small number were affiliated with other religious groups; only 518 had no religious affiliation.[12]

During Judge's training in Camp Travis, the Ninetieth Division intermixed Hispanics and Native American Indians with the non-Hispanic Caucasians.[13] It was probably the first exposure to minorities for Judge who had barely left Raymond, Minnesota. He probably caught his first glimpse of black men, too, as they were present at Camp Travis, assigned to a depot brigade.[14] Judge called them coons, an accepted term for blacks at the time. Even though he knew he was bound for another country overseas, the state of Texas may have already seemed like an exotic land to him.

Judge struck up a friendship with a fellow Minnesotan in his company named Richard F. Peters during his short training at Camp Travis. Richard was born in Cannon Falls, southeast of Minneapolis, in 1894.

The intense training period, consisting of basics such as trench warfare, marching, and weapons, was over in just five weeks. Judge was set to leave his country for the first time. He would be shipped overseas as part of the American Expeditionary Forces. The entire division would leave the United States through Camp Mills, Long Island, New York with the majority passing through England, and then on to France.

During his trip to New York, Judge wrote a letter home to his sister Etta. Still the farmboy, Judge notices the crops.

> *Saturday, June 8, 1918*
> *Dear Sis:*
>   *I was going to start this letter with a fountain pen, but it don't work. The train shakes too much. We are just going thru a town in Missouri named Aurora. It sure is some town. It looks like Raymond did before my time. Missouri looks so much like Minnesota in corn. The corn is only about a foot high. In Texas it is over my head. Some differ-ence, eh? This trip will take us about a week, so we have about four more days riding. But it sure is sport and soft because we have sleepers and tables and good things to eat. So what more does a hobo want! They turned the bunch lose in Paris, Texas yesterday and believe me we*

had some time with the Red Cross girls. They gave us everything anyone could wish for, even flowers.

So I suppose Bill is in France but this time helping the boys down the Beast of Berlin and I suppose Hank is probably on his way to New York, too.

Well Gettshee* it is a long way to berlin but we will get there yet. Uncle Sam will show the way by heck! It's raining like the dogs here now. But we have a roof over head so we will have to do like they do in Spain. Mr. Briggs** will tell you the rest. It is getting colder as we go east. It reminds me of Minnesota again. I see by the papers this morning the Germans are dying right and left. But what more can they expect when the American boys start shooting.

Well give my love to the whole family and tell them I am feeling fine and happy so good bye, I am missing good scenery by writing so will close.

Judge

Did my cloths get home

*nickname for Etta Knott

**minister who had revival meetings in Raymond

Everyone in the Ninetieth Division made it safely to France. Some ships carrying division personnel were attacked by lurking German U-boats, which infested the Atlantic Ocean looking for prey. But the division successfully thwarted the U-boat attacks with not a single loss of life due to hostilities.

Judge's world had suddenly become a dangerous place.

Judge at Camp Travis, Texas; May 1918; family photo.

View of Camp Travis looking toward Division Headquarters. Tents in foreground are part of old Camp Wilson, a National Guard mobilization camp

Camp Travis, Texas c. 1918, note the baseball field with bleachers on the right; photo from the *History of the 90th Division.*

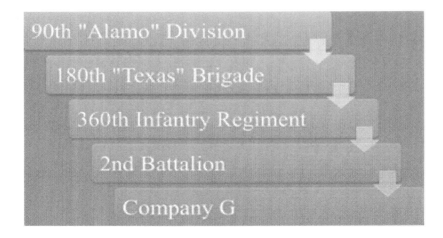

Judge Knott's Units: This graph illustrates Judge Knott's units from large to small. The Alamo division contained two infantry brigades, the 179th "Oklahoma" Brigade and the 180th "Texas" Brigade (it also contained the 165th Field Artillery, engineers and three machine gun battalions). The Texas Brigade contained two infantry regiments, the 359th and 360th. The 360th Infantry contained three battalions. Each battalion contained four companies. Typically, World War I divisions had around 25,000 men; brigades about 8,000 men; regiments contained 3,500 men; battalions about 800; companies about 180. The numbers greatly fluctuated during the war due to casualties, illness, reassignments, and replacements. Judge seemed to identify the most with his company, then division.

Ninetieth Division symbol of red T and O; cover of the *History of the 90th Division* book.

"Sable" on the cover of the 360th Infantry history book.

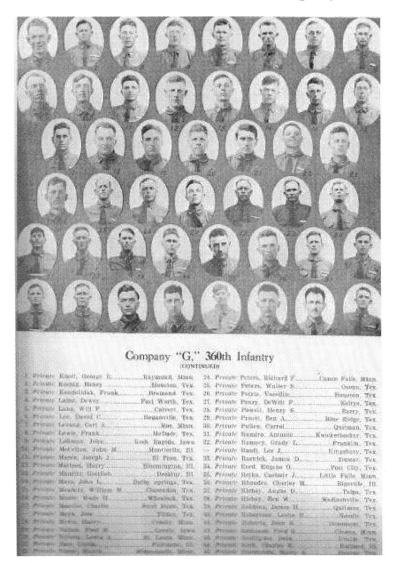

Judge is numbered 1 (top row far left); Richard Peters is numbered 24 (fourth row from top far left); from the 360th Infantry history book.

When wilt Thou save the people? O God of mercy, when?
Not kings and lords, but nations! Not thrones and crowns, but
men!
Flowers of Thy heart, O God, are they; Let them not pass, like
weeds away
Their heritage a sunless day, God save the people!

When Wilt Thou Save the People, hymn by Ebenezer Elliot,
from Judge's 1911 *The Methodist Sunday School Hymnal*

4 – Over There

Forty-three divisions of the American Expeditionary Forces (AEF) were sent to Europe. Judge's Ninetieth Division was the twenty-second to arrive *over there* in France.

The total loss of life during the four years of war was staggering, difficult to comprehend to this day.

About 4.8 million people from the United States served in the armed forces in the Great War; of that total just over 2 million did so overseas. About 1.4 million Americans fought in France.[1] Of those American soldiers who reached France, two out of three took part in battle.

In researching a documentary called *The Great War And the Shaping of the 20th Century*, PBS compiled casualty and death data from a variety of sources.[2] Exact figures may never be known due to inconsistent recording systems and definitions, and the loss of documentation over the years.

According to their calculations, about 117,000 Americans died due to battle deaths and disease during the 19 months the United States was in the war. US casualties (including wounded) were well over 320,000 men, 7 percent of the total casualties of the Allied forces.

The American numbers were simply unprecedented. By contrast, the United States had just over two million men fight in the Civil War over a four-year period.

The numbers were shockingly worse for some of the US Allies, with the British Empire sending nearly nine million soldiers and France sending about eight and a half million. Russian soldiers numbered twelve million, with a horrific nine million casualties, comprising 76 percent of the casualty rate for the Allied forces. Total number of men fighting for the Allies was just over 40 million with a 52 percent casualty rate.

The grim figures were even more wretched for the losing side. Germany and the Central powers saw 65 million men go to war with a 57 percent casualty rate.

"The war to end all wars" became a delusional catchphrase during the war. The utter destruction was so terrifyingly evil it had to be somehow justified. In America, the war had come to be considered an extremely unpleasant but necessary task to make the world safe for democracy. It would be done and over with. To repeat it was unthinkable, some thought, the often-cited definition of insanity. However, at least one person may not have agreed: an Austrian-born soldier fighting for the Germans by the name of Adolf Hitler.

Some units of the US Ninetieth Division sailed directly to France, however, most passed through England, docking in Liverpool or Southampton by late June and July. Then, they crossed the English Channel to Cherbourg or Le Havre.

Judge, along with the entire 360th sailed from New York aboard the *Olympic* on June 14 to Southampton, arriving June 22. The *Olympic* also carried the division commander, General Henry T. Allen, and many troops from other divisions as well.[3] As of July 1, Judge was promoted to private first class and soon after earned twenty dollars allotment per month, minus the six dollars and fifty cents for $10,000 worth of war risk insurance.

The US soldiers were called Sammies (after Uncle Sam), Yanks, and Doughboys. Judge's hometown newspaper *The Raymond News* frequently called them Yanks. Doughboy was the moniker that stuck once they hit French soil. The most widely-accepted theory for the nickname came from the spherical US uniform buttons that resembled dough dumplings, although other explanations exist.

Upon arrival in France, the 360th Infantry set up its headquarters in Rouvres-sur-Aube, after a lengthy railroad boxcar trip of approximately thirty hours. Railway stations attracted large crowds when the American newspapers arrived, which were distributed by the Red Cross and YMCA. Everyone was eager for news of the fighting as they sensed their time at the battlefront was imminent.

At the time, the war, which had been going on in Europe since 1914, had largely resulted in a bitter stalemate early on along a line called the Western Front. East of Germany, Russia had dropped out of the fighting. When Judge arrived, the Germans were making a last desperate attempt on the Marne River to get into Paris, just before a French counterattack that marked the turning of the war in favor of the Allied forces.

The Ninetieth Division was joined by seventeen experienced French officers who helped train the men for five weeks in the new techniques of warfare. The French training officers were part of the so-called French Mission, including a captain named Naulet of the 114th Battalion of Chasseurs. Captain Naulet served with the Texas Brigade during most of the upcoming battle period.[4] After training the doughboys, the French officers facilitated relations with the civilian population and insured liaison with French units. The French word "liaison" was quickly adopted by the Americans. Liaison was originally used by the French as a cooking term meaning to bind together.

The new recruits trained eight hours a day in trenching, target practice, bayonet exercises, drills, maneuvers and tactics. In July, Judge attended gas school in Aulnoy. While the newly-enlisted

American men learned what they could in such a short time, many of their officers had little or no war experience as well.

On August 15, 1918 they went through a regulating station at Pagny-sur-Meuse and were told their destination. The Ninetieth Division learned they had been sent to relieve the First Division, which had literally been the first US division to enter battle in the war earlier in that year. By August 18, the 360th Infantry was in Domgermain.

Just before his first taste of battle at the front line, Judge wrote a letter home, eager to learn about his brothers. Bill, with the Eighty-second Division, was already in France.

> *Tuesday, August 21, 1918*
> *Dear Folks at home*
> *Dear Sister:*
> *Well I have a few minutes off so will take advantage of it and write. Send me Bill and Ten's addresses please so I could probably be able to locate them. I am having a good time at present and still happy and well, and sure do hope this reaches you the same. So say hello to all the boys if there are any left for me and tell them to not worry because I won't take long before we are with them. Will write more next time, because I am not in a very good condition to write at present.*
> *Love to all,*
> *Judge*
> *P.S. I make an allotment for twenty dollars a month start-ing the first of Aug.*

Judge's cousin, Carlton Knott, wrote his mother Bertha about this time. He, too, was curious on the whereabouts of his brother Ray, and cousins Judge, Ten, and Will.

> *Dearest Mother Mine:*

How is Mother? I hope you are as well off as I am, for I'm getting fatter and lazier every day and I sure am feeling fine. This climate has everything beat I ever heard of. Just like a man would order it, to live, eat and sleep and grow fat.

I was out and had a bill of wild black berries yesterday and am going again today as it is Sunday and that means liberty day.

I am trying to learn French, but it is some talk, all I can say is "Good Morning and Good Night." And a couple more little things like that.

I haven't heard from Ray yet, in fact I haven't heard from any one for a month and for all I know there may not be any U.S.A. A person would think by the looks here that the U.S.A. has moved over here, Ha Ha.

If you know where uncle Will's boys are, let me know the Co. and Regiment they are in. I may be able to find them, but I can't find out a thing about where Ray is, no more than when I was there.

They are threshing around here now. Some threshing rig too. They all hand feed and they put it in careful, heads first and all the heads on one side so the straw doesn't get broken up so much. It comes out just about the way it goes in, only the grain is all out of it.

Well Mother mine, don't worry about me. I'm O.K. and couldn't be better off anywhere. Tell Sis (Pearl I mean) to write or I won't own her as a sister any more and--won't like her anymore, Ha Ha. Well bye, bye.
With love from your son,
Carlton

Two reoccurring themes emerged from the letters written home to Minnesota by the Knott boys. First, they reassured everyone they were safe, urging everyone at home not to worry. The second theme was a longing desire to see or learn news about each other while serving in the war.

The Ninetieth Division was spread out over five and half miles of front during this time. The 360th relieved the Twenty-sixth Infantry of the First Division. It was located just north of Toul near the Moselle River. Pont-a-Mousson was to the right of the 360th.

The infantry regiment was divided into three battalions. Each battalion (about 900 to 1000 men) contained four companies. Judge's Company G was assigned to the Second Battalion. The three battalions acted as a team to accomplish their objectives during the war. Often, two battalions would take their turn on the front line, while the other attempted to rest in reserve, although being in reserve often meant still being in range of German shells.

During this period and only under the cover of darkness, the men cleaned out the old French trenches of trash and barbed wire. Thousands of old French grenades littered the trenches. The Ninetieth Division saw its first casualties of the war when two soldiers were killed by the accidental discharge of a discarded French hand grenade during the night of August 24. Until September 12, battle casualties for the division totaled ten fatalities, thirty-nine wounded and one missing.[5]

In late August, rumors were circulating of an upcoming US offensive. Activities were kept quiet and under cover. After four years of war, the seasoned French civilians knew something was imminent, more so than the inexperienced doughboys.[6] Throughout the days of preparation for the US offensive, the farmers of Villers-en-Haye continued to calmly work their fields.[7]

War materials and supplies were stashed anywhere they could be. "There was not a nook or cranny, in the woods, behind a ridge, under the cover of a quarry, that did not conceal a battery, a tank, an ammunition dump, a depot of engineering supplies," the division historian Major George Wythe wrote in *A History of the 90th Division*. "The huge Foret (forest) de Puvenelle, which seemed to cover half the divisional area, was alive with the materials of war."

At night, muddy roads were jammed with artillery, trucks, horse transport, automobiles, tanks, motorcycle messengers, and marching troops. No lights were allowed.

Then, on the evening of September 11, 1918, the infantry assembled in the pouring rain. "The night was black as ink and the rain was coming down in sheets," Wyeth wrote.

The 360th marched to a new position, now certain something was about to happen.

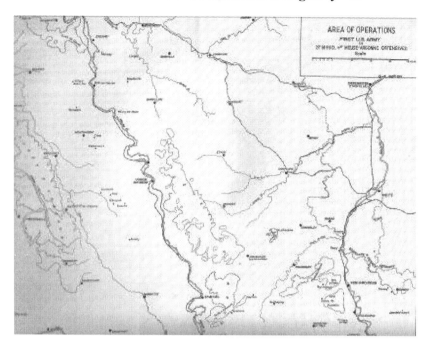

Map of the operational area in France, from *A History Of The 90th Division.*

I shall not fear the battle If Thou art by my side,
Nor wander from the pathway If Thou wilt be my guide.

O Jesus, I Have Promised, 1866 hymn by John E. Bode,
from Judge's 1911 *The Methodist Sunday School Hymnal*

5 – Over The Top At St. Mihiel

The American Expeditionary Forces were the first American army ever sent to Europe. The war brought an unprecedented change in US foreign policy and outlook, a transformation from isolationism to involvement. The distinguishing aspect of the battle of St. Mihiel is that it became the first time that the AEF operated as an independent army.[1] Until then, the American forces augmented the French and British Allied troops and were ultimately under their direction. That was to change on September 12, 1918.

The AEF, under command of General John J. Pershing, was now to fight as an equal Allied partner under their own command. St. Mihiel was the largest US battle to date since the Civil War.

The St. Mihiel offensive was the long-awaited, highly-anticipated big American push hoped for by the Allies and dreaded by the Germans. The valuable French land of the St. Mihiel area possessed strategic advantages—its elevated geography and its supply connections from Nancy to Paris and Verdun. It was one of the first areas taken by the Germans earlier in the war. The French had unsuccessfully and repeatedly attempted to regain the land at great human cost.

At the beginning of the offensive, the Germans were in the early stages of a pull out of the area to strengthen their defensive backup position known as the Hindenburg Line. Most of the area's perimeter belonged to the Allies and it became too difficult and risky for the Germans to defend. They had to get out while the getting was good. Still, the Germans were taken by surprise, advantage: Allies.

Generally, the AEF and French divisions did not experience intense fighting. However, German pockets of resistance--some with gas attacks--were met by the Ninetieth Division. It had been raining for days resulting in filthy, swampy conditions. Mud, barbed wire, lice, and rats were inescapable.

The Ninetieth Division was placed between the Fifth Division on its left and the Eighty-second Division (with Judge's brother Bill) on its right. Even though Bill was with an engineering regiment, two of the Knott boys were "fighting" side by side, but did not know it at the time. Just right of the Eighty-second Division, which was the far right flank of the attack, was the Moselle River, which marked the eastern border of the offensive. St. Mihiel marked the western point.

The occupying Germans knew the area extremely well. Opposing the US Ninetieth Division were the German 255th Infantry Division, and elements of the German 77th Reserve Division that included many green Prussian replacements. The German 255th, however, contained mostly older, experienced men from the Alsace Lorraine area who had been in the sector since the unit's formation in 1917.[2]

US intelligence learned all they could about the whereabouts of German units before the offensive began. The location of German strong points, trenches, machine gun and trench mortar positions, camps, roads, and supply depots all needed to be noted. It was of utmost importance to the infantry that this key life-saving informa-tion be known, so the US artillery barrage could be effective before they attacked on foot. German prisoners and deserters also provided US intelligence with the German order of battle and troop strength.[3]

The 360th Infantry Regiment had two of its three battalions in line on day one. Judge's Second Battalion was in reserve in the northern edge of Foret de Puvenelle, where the copious amounts of supplies and equipment were stashed. The first day's objective was met, but a German counterattack was feared that night.

During the night, Judge and the Second Battalion was released from division reserve and passed through the First Battalion to take up position in the notorious Bois le Pretre (priest's woods), one of the bloodiest sites of the war. In 1915, the French attacked for months, hoping to progress toward the Moselle River, only to gain yards of territory. Later, the Germans counterattacked and reclaimed the area.

When the stalemate later occurred, the opposing trenches were so close, anything above a whisper could be heard by the enemy.[4] Gradually, the No Man's Land widened as they both pulled their lines back, leaving behind a maze of abandoned trenches and barbed wire. The dense forest of the Bois le Pretre had been pulverized into a field of stumps.

The Second and Third Battalions were selected from the 360th to make an attack and seize all the high ground south of the Trey Valley. Just beyond the woods were quarries west of the town of Norroy, which were particularly feared due to previous failed French attempts against the Germans. The Germans had held and fortified the land for four years.

Plans to attack the seemingly impregnable Norroy Quarries had not been included in the St. Mihiel offensive's objectives. Instead, they were to be "dealt with by exploitation", according to the division history by Wythe. On September 12, US heavy artillery was ordered to prepare the way, and gas troops had been provided as well.

The artillery, while helpful in bolstering the confidence of the infantrymen, was largely unable to make a large impression on the German defenses who were encased in mined dugouts forty feet deep.[5] Plus, the US gas troops fell through due to an accidental explosion which killed some of its men. Fortunately, the infantrymen were blissfully ignorant of these setbacks.

At 7:00 a.m. on September 13th, Judge climbed out of the trenches and went over the top for the first time, advancing northeast toward the quarries. Their battle cry going over the top was their regimental yell,

The bear jumped over the panther bluff, hell fire and a fuzzy-O!

The Second and Third Battalions moved in tandem. Progress was slow and strongly opposed by German machine guns protected by concrete structures. The doughboys now became painfully aware the German machine gunners had not been sufficiently softened up by the Ninetieth Division's artillery preparation prior to their foot attack.

Yet, by the end of the most difficult day yet, the two battalions prevailed.

According to Wythe, the capture of Norroy Quarries was the "greatest advance" of September 13th and one of the regiment's "brilliant achievements" during the war.

" . . . Overcoming machine gun resistance, and ignoring the bursting of high explosives, the two battalions occupied and thoroughly mopped up the quarries by 5 p.m.," Wythe wrote.

The doughboys now controlled the dreaded Bois le Pretre (priest's woods) and Norroy Quarries. In addition, the 360th captured large quantities of medical supplies, machine gun parts, and ammunition. Among the spoils were minenwerfer (light mortars), gas projectors, grenades, telephone repair kits, signal outfits, rations and equipment. The German dugouts, which were hastily abandoned, felt luxurious to the doughboys. The victorious Americans occupied the fully-equipped offices, furnished dining rooms, and recreations rooms with pianos.

Judge's daughter, Mildred, described the deserted German dugouts. "They went in for the night. The soldiers collapsed in exhaustion on the floor. Judge wanted to cheer them up. He looked upstairs and found a long nightgown one of the German officers must have worn. He put it on, went downstairs and put on a show.

He said the other soldiers were rolling on the floor and laughing so hard that their sides hurt."

The Bois le Pretre (priest's woods) and Norroy Quarries victory was considered the 360th most outstanding feat of arms during World War I, according to the regiment's organized reserves that formed after the war. In 1925, it developed a 360th unit insignia and military coat of arms that depicts Sable the bear mascot and a tree with barbed wire around the trunk.[6] The tree symbolizes the Bois-le-Pretre and its capture on September 13, 1918. The star represents Texas, the Lone Star State. The Ninetieth Division's red T and O are also present.

On September 15 the First Battalion was to advance to a new outpost at Cote 327, about a mile north of the quarries near the town of Vandieres. Patrols from the Second and Third Battalions were sent out to pave the way. During one dangerous patrol, a detachment from Judge's Company G entered the trenches on the east edge of Bois (woods) de la Rappes and killed a number of Germans. As a result of the patrols, the First Battalion was able to advance without facing machine gun fire.

The neighboring Eighty-second Division with Judge's brother Bill, meanwhile, had not advanced as the Ninetieth. So, the 360th Infantry established posts west of the Moselle River in Vandieres, on the night of September 16. As a result, the 360th had two "front" lines, doubling their exposure to attack, one at their front and the second at their right flank.

Soon after the St. Mihiel offensive, Judge wrote his sister Etta. It was his first letter home after going over the top.

> *September 21, 1918*
> *Somewhere in France*
> *Dear Sis:*
> *Well kid I am just going to write a few lines to let the bunch know I am still living and feeling fine. We went over*

the top and came out with grand success. Will write more
when I get in a position to do so.
With love to all
Judge

After the war, Judge told his daughter Mildred he remembered standing in the trenches with "rats running everywhere."

"The rats were a mixed blessing as they could smell the threat of gas. Once, Daddy said a voice inside told him to immediately get out of a foxhole.[7] He jumped out after warning the others. Some followed. One soldier was just coming out when a mortar landed in the foxhole and blew his head off," Mildred recounted. Judge heard and heeded the urgent voice inside him a couple of times during the war, which he later believed saved his life more than once.

After the battle of St. Mihiel, the AEF silenced any doubts that they could fight on their own. The victory was a huge morale booster. They had proven themselves, but a tougher test was soon to come.

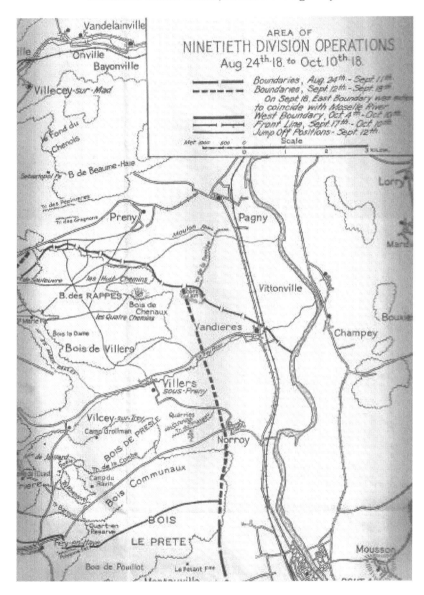

Map from *A History Of The 90th Division.*

View of the region which was No Man's Land before the attack on September 12, taken from jump-off trenches in front of Fey-en-Haye. The assaulting battalions were forced to cross the maze of trenches and wire before getting at grips with the enemy

Photo from the *History of the 90th Division.*

360th insignia developed after the war.

So prepare, say a prayer,
Send the word, send the word to beware;
We'll be over, we're coming over,
And we won't come back 'til it's over, over there

Over There, 1917 song by George M. Cohan

6 – "I Am Trying My Best To Shoot-Them"

During the evening of September 16, the 360th had reached about 330 yards southwest of the town of Pagny-sur-Moselle in France. It was the end of the forward movement. Daytime patrols ordered to reconnoiter had encountered German machine gun fire and little progress was made. The effort now concentrated on the organization of the sector.

The period of September 16 through October 10 became a time for the Ninetieth Division to hold position until relief came by the Seventh Division. While it was a period of stabilization, it was none-the-less an extremely trying period for the doughboys.[1]

While the infantrymen were tired after four days of combat, they still needed to both defend their newly-acquired land and perform much needed manual labor to fortify their new front.

The supply company also hustled to provide hot meals and water to the soldiers. They were dangerously near the front lines, often under fire from German shells. Supply men, and even their horses, were killed in the line of duty while feeding the infantrymen. The Germans knew the area after living there for four years and would shell the spring water sources where they knew the K.P. (kitchen police) would be.[2]

Ammunition was restocked and telephone wires were laid. Engineers went to work rebuilding the roads that were a muddy, shell-pocked mess. Barbed wire needed to be cleared and reset, old trenches filled, and new ones dug. Throughout this exhaustive work, they were continually exposed to heavy shelling by the Germans.

Clean clothes were provided at Griscourt and the ragged doughboys needed to bathe and de-louse. Many uniforms were in shreds from fighting through the barbed wire. For the men, it seemed an agonizingly long wait to get cleaned up. They re-drilled to emphasize discipline.

On October 4, the front widened for the Ninetieth Division. The Seventy-eighth Division had been on their left and had been ordered to pull out to prepare for another offensive west of the Meuse River. Some division replacements arrived October 6.

Patrols regularly went out to harass the Germans. Five miles west of where Judge was positioned, the Germans had saturated the area with mustard gas.[3] One hundred and fifty division men had to be evacuated. "The effects of the gas were horrible beyond description, some being blinded for life, others disfigured by the effects of the acid on parts of the skin which the liquid had touched. . . practically every man in the battalion, although continuing to do duty, was weakened by inhaling the fumes. . . As a result of the gas the men could not refrain from coughing, sentries on outpost duty sometimes giving away their position as a consequence," wrote Wythe in the division history book.

About this time, Judge became a runner in the war. Runners in World War I were responsible for memorizing and delivering messages by foot between units or between units and headquarters. It was an extremely dangerous job. Mildred explained how it came about.

"Daddy was a runner between the lines with messages. Some of the messengers were killed. So they chose other soldiers to take his place. They were given a message to memorize. The soldier who was accurate in remembering the message was the runner. He memorized the message with orders to kill anyone he met," she explained.

Once, she said Judge was running "in the open in what he called no-man's land. A German biplane spotted him and started yelling and shooting at him. It was so low that he could see the pilot's face. He ran faster, tripped and fell in a shell hole. They kept firing and then went away. I think they thought he was dead. He crawled out of the shell hole and ran to headquarters. It was so dangerous that sometimes he wished that his memory wasn't so good."

The harrowing biplane incident was described in more detail by Judge to his new son-in-law in 1963.

Dennis Zetah, who had just married Judge's daughter Elaine, was in the army and busy complaining to his father-in-law about army life. Dennis said he and Judge were sitting on a bench in Judge's yard in Raymond, Minnesota overlooking the skating rink when, "I started grousing about spending time at Camp McCoy."

"Was anybody shooting at you today?" Judge responded.

"No," Dennis replied.

"Well then, sounds like you had a pretty good day." Judge then went on to tell Dennis he was shot at by a German in a plane fifty years ago during the war.

"Plane?" Dennis asked, doubtful there were airplanes used in the First World War.

At that point, Dennis said Judge looked him straight in the eye with the most incredulous expression on his face. Then, Judge began recounting his days as a runner. "His good memory was to blame. He relayed the messages almost verbatim and he became a runner. The life expectancy of a runner was about seven to ten days," Dennis said.

On one dispatch in an area full of artillery shell holes, a German plane spotted the solitary Judge and began shooting to kill. Judge looked over his shoulder at the plane, tripped, and fell into a large shell hole, which was about fifteen feet wide by seven feet deep. The Germans had mounted machine guns on their planes, but the guns could not rotate or adjust their trajectory. That meant the planes had to point their nose at a precise angle and fly straight at their target.

Lucky for Judge, the side of the deep shell hole provided cover. But, the plane made a U-turn and came back shooting. Meanwhile, Judge had quickly crawled to the far side of the crater and clung to the opposite side, knowing he would be protected from the bullets coming from that angle and direction. Then, the German pilot gave up. Judge said the pilot was wearing a scarf.

On another message run, Mildred said Judge encountered a lone German soldier. In an act of mercy, Judge did not kill him, despite orders to do so.

"Once, Judge was running through the woods and saw a young German soldier sitting on a stump. The German held up his arms and cried 'mercy' and 'mother'. Daddy said that he couldn't kill him as all he thought about was going home to his mother. He talked about that soldier all through his life and hoped that he made it home," Mildred said.

By October 10, 1918, the Seventh Division had arrived to relieve the Ninetieth Division. They then traveled as quickly as they could about fifty miles west . . . not to rest but to prepare to jump off in the Meuse-Argonne offensive, which had already begun. In cold, torrential rains, they trucked to Blercourt, about seven miles west of Verdun. By October 16, Judge and the Texas Brigade arrived and were billeted in barracks at nearby Jouy, Rampont, and neighboring camps.

Judge finally found time and a clean, dry place to write home after the battle of St. Mihiel. He wrote on a Sunday, after attending chapel service. He mentions his sisters Etta, Effie, Emma, Grace and Jeanette, his younger brother Roy (Punk), his brother-in-law Charlie, and his girlfriend Ruby. He also mentions Jake Haima who owned Haima's Store in Raymond, and Jake's son, John. Again, he seemed eager to learn news of his brothers in France.

October 20, 1918

Dear Mother,
Dear Folks at home:

Well it is raining out so I guess I will have time to scribble a few lines to let you know that I am fine and dandy on October 20. The chapel had a meeting this morning over in our barracks. We sang a few songs like the ones we sing in our church in Raymond. So Etta is clerking in Haima's store. I wonder if she and John ever get in a fight and does old Jake get hardboiled when business is bad. Bill and Ten is somewhere in France, but where is more than I can say. They might be ten miles from me or a hundred. I sure would like to run across them here. It would seem almost like getting home once more. I suppose Punk will be the next one in France. Then almost the whole family will be here. Do any of you know if Ben Miller* is in the next draft with Punk? I got a letter from Grace and Jeanette yesterday and was glad to hear that everything is all right at home. Grace is teaching the Dutchmen** and I am trying my best to shoot them. Effie wrote and told me she is going to shoot a bear and make a rug. I think she had better teach those brats of hers and leave bears alone. Jeanette was telling me about Miller's Elevator burning down. I wonder if the Elevator Company will build another one in Raymond, or he might have to move to have another one to run. Did Emma or Charlie sell out their place in Benson or did they rent it out? And Emma wants Punk to get baptized before he goes in the Army. I wonder if she thinks that will stop a bullet. I get two letters from Ruby almost every week. That is more than I get from home, and also more than she gets from me. But I am not always in a position to write like the rest of you are. She wrote and told me she was going to send me a Xmas present in the same package I got from home, because we can only get one package per man. I will send some presents if I ever get back to a civi-

lized place in France where a fellow can buy something.
Well I hope this will find you all happy and well. I remain
your loving son.
Judge

*Ben Miller was a friend from Raymond
**Judge used the term *Dutchmen* to mean Deutsche or German men

Another letter soon followed.

Monday, October 28, 1918
Dear Mother:
I received a letter home day before yesterday so it is up to me to answer the same. I am feeling fine these days so I surely hav'nt anything to kick about in that direction. I hope that Kaiser will soon see that he had better stop while stopping is good or before long he might wake up missing. I think I walked right by Ten the other night. But I didn't know it till the other day. Now we are some ways apart. I sure was glad to get Etta's letter, because she gave me the good news about the Raymond boys being all rare and go. I sure wish you would send me the Raymond News once in awhile. The rest of the boys get papers every week or so from home. Is Punk in the Army yet? I bet his is having some time these days because he is chief cook and bottle washer of the ranch. So the kid is rushing Eva Nelson from Whitefield.* Tell the kid he had better pick on somebody his size. She could easily take him down and sit on him. Send me all the Raymond boys addresses so I probably can find a few of them. Well I can't tell you much about anything of army life, where we are or what we are going to do, because Mr. Censor will have the bother of cutting it out. Hoping this letter finds you all in the best of spirits. I remain your son.

Love to all,
Judge
*rushing was a popular term for courting

It would be a few weeks before Judge was able to write home again. Those weeks would bring his most intense experience of war.

street of Blercourt. This town was the headquarters of the 90th Division from October 13 to October 19, when the Division was moving into the Meuse-Argonne sector

[79]

Photo from the *History of the 90th Division.*

Illustration from *A Short History and Photographic Record of the 360th Infantry Texas Brigade.*

The Lord is my shepherd; I shall not want.
He maketh me to lie down in green pastures:
he leadeth me beside the still waters.
He restoreth my soul:
he leadeth me in the paths of righteousness for his name's sake.
Yea, though I walk through the valley of the shadow of death, I
will fear no evil:
for thou art with me; thy rod and thy staff they comfort me.
Thou preparest a table before me in the presence of mine
enemies:
thou anointest my head with oil; my cup runneth over.
Surely goodness and mercy shall follow me all the days of my
life:
and I will dwell in the house of the Lord for ever.

Psalm 23 (KJV)

7 – The Battle Of Meuse-Argonne

Meanwhile, the AEF had already begun the largest US Army battle to date: the Meuse-Argonne. On September 26, French and US divisions had begun a huge offensive bordered by the Argonne Forest on the west and the Meuse River on the east. The site picked was a controversial area near dreaded Verdun, which had been a site of intense carnage for the French earlier in the war. They had no desire to return for more.

The St. Mihiel and Meuse-Argonne offensives were to be fought in quick succession, something that was unprecedented for the United States and difficult to accomplish logistically to say the least. Some 450,000 men had to be transported within days or weeks from the St. Mihiel area. A total of 1.25 million men took part, including all three of the Knott brothers and one Knott cousin, Carlton.

Prominent Americans who fought in the Meuse-Argonne were Douglas MacArthur, Billy Mitchell, George Patton, Harry Truman and Alvin York (part of the Eighty-second Division with Judge's brother Bill). George C. Marshall planned the attack.

The size of infantry companies had shrunk, due to war casualties and the Spanish Influenza pandemic, which ended up killing an estimated 30-50 million people worldwide by the time it subsided in 1919.[1] One in four men in the army were influenza victims. Many developed pneumonia and died within a week.

The Ninetieth Division entered the front with the 179th Oklahoma Brigade on October 22 during the second phase of the battle. Judge and the 180th Texas Brigade, in reserve in Jouy and Rampont, moved up to Bois de Cuisy. It was the division policy to designate one brigade to attack, with the other in reserve. The reserve brigade would take over when heavy casualties and utter exhaustion made it necessary.

The Eighty-ninth Division was on their left. On the right was initially the Third Division and later the Fifth. The Ninetieth Division occupied the front near the eastern flank, as in the St. Mihiel, closer to the Meuse River than the Argonne Forest.

The Texas Brigade set up headquarters at Nantillois under Brig. Gen. Ulysses McAlexander, a Minnesota native. The area was continually shelled by the Germans, despite the brigade being in reserve behind the front. Some reserve men were wounded and killed. Division chaplains conducted burials as the shells exploded around them.[2]

Still present were the mud and rats. The weather had turned colder. Rain and sleet fell.

The Oklahoma Brigade's objective was to establish a jump-off point for the Texas Brigade on November 1, confronting the German position called the Freya Stellung. It was the third part of the Hindenburg Line, a succession of three defensive positions, named Giselher, Kriemhilde, and Freya, three witches from operas by German composer Richard Wagner.

The Texas Brigade was to deliver the attack on November 1. They were brought up to the front during the night of October 30-31 to become familiar with the terrain. This was key for the field artillery, as they were to deliver a bombardment the very next night preceding the infantry attack. Precision during this bombardment was crucial; it was a vunerable point in time where both relieving and relieved brigades would simultaneously be at the forward zone in the dark. Luckily, the relief was made without a casualty.[3]

The stage was set for a face off between the Texas Brigade and the Germans during the final phase of the Meuse-Argonne offensive. Weakened in size, the Texas Brigade was operating at only 50 percent for officers and 65 percent for enlisted men.[4]

According to the brigade intelligence, the terrain was not a maze of trenches the doughboys encountered at the St. Mihiel offensive. Instead, there were concrete-fortified German machine gun pits, some barbed wire, and foxholes. Foxholes, or funk holes as they were sometimes called during World War I, were individual pits dug at scattered intervals for protection against shell fire.[5]

Opposite the under-strength Texas boys were two regiments of the German Eighty-eighth Division on the west, three regiments of the notorious Twenty-eighth "Kaiser's Favorite" Division in the middle, and one regiment of the 107th Division on the east flank.[6] The Kaiser's Favorite Division held most of the sector.

Heavy German artillery fire began at midnight, Halloween night, against the entire regimental sector, just before the American bombardment was set to begin at 3:30 in the morning on November 1. Unfortunately, cover for the doughboys was lacking and heavy casualties were inflicted.

"Huge quantities of thermite – it almost seemed to be liquid fire at the time – were showered upon the three battalions . . . Another shell touched off the regiment's pile of pyrotechnics in a dump near headquarters and sent a shower of colored lights into the air. The spectacle was viewed for miles, and soon runners were everywhere attempting to learn the meaning of the confusion of signals. One of the flares set off was the one to announce that the corps' objective had been reached, and more than one officer along the line was puzzled at its appearance, for there still remained hours before the men were to go over the top," according to *A History Of The Activities And Operations Of The 360th United States Infantry Regiment In The World War, 1914-1918.*[7]

Then, at 3:30 a.m. the American artillery began its reply. For the Texas Brigade, H hour was 5:30 a.m. The 360th Infantry's Second and Third Battalions were to lead the forward attack, with the First in reserve.

Judge's Company G with the Second Battalion went over the top, with the Third Battalion taking the lead.

"No sooner had the assaulting wave debouched from its cover when a terrific machine gun fire poured into the lines . . . Despite the thoroughness of our magnificent artillery barrage, many enemy gunners found cover in the shelters in the vicinity of the farm and came to the surface again in time to catch the advancing infantry," wrote Wyeth.

The Germans were once again taken by surprise. But, this time they bitterly and skillfully defended their heavily fortified lines. They had occupied the area for four years and were exceptionally prepared to meet the enemy.

The Germans were determined to hold every inch to protect fellow divisions that were retreating from the Laon salient into Germany. They also wanted to protect their strategic railroad near Sedan. The US Ninetieth Division encountered Germans that were first-class soldiers and resistant to the death.[7] The doughboys encountered extremely heavy machine gun fire.

According to plans, their first objective was to take Hills 300 and 278, and the Cheline Ravine by 8:00 a.m. Once done, they were to move north to northeast of Andevanne and a ridge west to Croix St. Mouclen. After that, on day two, there was no set pace. They were to exploit and advance as far as possible.

The jump off point was just north of a road leading northwest from Bantheville where it loops around the northeastern corner of Bois de Bantheville. The hills were soon captured and they waited thirty minutes to catch their breath.

By 8:30 am, three ghastly attempts to advance by the Third Battalion were thwarted by the Germans. At noon, Judge and the Second Battalion were ordered to take up the advance, led by Major Hall Etter, who had been a regimental adjutant at Camp Travis. They maneuvered west through Bois d'Andrevanne to avoid open ground, which was being swept by enemy fire, then moved forward into Bois Capiere, north of Andrevanne. The rapid advance was so effective that enemy machine gunners were captured in position together with their guns. The Third Battalion followed.

At darkness, the Second Battalion reached the railroad running though the woods from Cote 243. The First Battalion, using compasses to guide them at night, received orders to pass through the Second to seize Cote 243.

US artillery fire was still landing on Cote 243 when they arrived at the woods, but was quickly halted through telephone communication with regimental headquarters. Judge and the Second Battalion were right behind the First.

At 1:30 p.m., the Second Battalion resumed the lead toward Chassogne Farm, which had been decimated by artillery fire and offered no cover whatsoever. Initially, the exposed battalion found itself under heavy machine gun fire from all sides. Fortunately, darkness crept in. With it came welcome news from patrols that the Germans were falling back toward Villers.

The big attack was a complete success!

Not only were all of the first day's objectives met, the 360th had smashed through the Freya Stellung. With that last push, the infamous Hindenburg Line had been pierced. Other US divisions had been successful in advancing, too; the enemy's last major line of resistance had collapsed.[8]

According to the regiment history book, the November 1 advancement by the 360th "ranks not only as its greatest perform-ance in the war, but as one of the most telling assaults delivered by any organization of troops on the entire Western Front.

"When the second battalion had broken the Freya Stellung, that last hope of the now-despairing Germans had been shattered. The success of this regiment had been duplicated by most of the regiments of other divisions in line to the right and left, and the succeeding division and corps' orders indicated that the gigantic German war machine which had fought so brilliantly for more than four years, was fast crumbling." [10]

On November 2, day two, the Texas Brigade, without much rest, was once again ordered to push the advance, this time to the bluffs of Halles/Mont-devant/Sassey. Again, they met heavy machine gun fire from the Germans. The 360th on Cote 243 was being fired upon from Cote 321 (just north of Villers-devant-Dun) and from the Bois de Raux.

To clean out the two areas, US artillery fire was ordered in preparation for attack. By 1:30 p.m., the Third Battalion passed the Second and proceeded to the Bois de Raux. The First Battalion moved on Cote 321 and met bitter opposition.

The Texas Brigade had suffered heavy casualties and was near exhaustion by November 3, day three. At the same time, many Germans had been killed or taken prisoner. During the previous two days, 180 German officers and 789 enlisted men were taken prisoner, a large majority of whom were taken by the 360th. The Oklahoma Brigade was ordered to relieve the Texas boys. The Germans were now in retreat.

On November 3, the Oklahoma Brigade advanced to the Meuse River and was surprised to find no resistance as the Germans had already crossed the river. Until November 7, the Oklahoma Brigade held the line along the Meuse. Judge and the Texas Brigade continued in reserve in Bois de Montigny.

Being in reserve, however, did not mean they were out of range, out of danger, and could relax. High casualties during this time testified to the deadly accuracy of the German artillery, which often targeted rear areas, roads and water sources. Some men actually felt safer at the front line. Shrapnel produced from the German shells came from all directions when explosions occurred. Even trees became impaling splinter projectiles. Machine gun bullets, by comparison, inflicted a more "clean" wound.

It was a period of great suffering for the doughboys. They were nearly spent, many were unfit for duty. And, their hygienic condition could only be described as disgusting due to the foul conditions, diarrhea, and body lice.

In the *History of the 90th Division*, Wythe described the situation. "The physical condition of the men of the 360th Infantry was very serious at this time. The physical strain of the severe fighting in piercing the Freya Stellung; the damp, unhealthy surroundings in which they found themselves in the Bois de Montigny, without sufficient blankets or overcoats, as all packs had not yet been brought up; impure water and cold meals at uncertain hours – these were some of the circumstances which made nearly forty percent of the regiment victims of diarrhea, and twenty percent patients with sub-acute bronchitis."

All three battalions were sent to somewhat better quarters in the morning of November 7. Judge, along with the Second Battalion, was sent down to Bantheville. Two days later on the afternoon of November 9, they received orders to cross the Meuse River.

On the morning of November 10, the Texas Brigade crossed the river at Dun-sur-Meuse. While they crossed, they received news that Germany's Kaiser Wilhelm II had abdicated. The end of the war was now in sight.

Although rumors of an armistice had been circulating for weeks, Judge had no way of knowing it was to come that very next day, and the Americans continued their momentum in defeating the Germans. The fighting on November 10 was severe and costly. In the division, one officer and 33 enlisted men were killed and 12 officers and 171 men were wounded.

"It is probable that no other division in the Expeditionary Forces met with such stubborn resistance during the last hours preceding the cessation of hostilities," Wythe wrote.

The last early morning orders for the Texas Brigade on November 11 were to advance in liaison with the Eighty-ninth Division to the heights overlooking the Chiers River. Before daylight, two battalions of the 360th were ready to advance toward Mouzay; the Second in support of the First. The Third Battalion was in reserve.

That evening, the Germans severely gassed Mouzay, Judge's destination, despite the presence of about six hundred civilians. Some men from the Texas Brigade had to be evacuated.

Then, on November 11, 1918, news of an armistice reached division headquarters at 7:20 a.m. The bulletin read:

1. You are informed that hostilities will cease along the whole front at 11 hours on November 11, 1918, Paris time.

2. No allied troops will pass the line reached by them at that hour and date until further orders.

3. All communication with the enemy, both before and after the termination of hostilities, is absolutely forbidden. In case of violation of this order the severest disciplinary measures will be immediately taken. Any officer offending will be sent to these headquarters under guard.

4. Every emphasis will be laid on the fact that the arrangement is an armistice only, and not a peace.

5. There must not be the slightest relaxation of vigilance. The troops must be prepared any moment for further operations. Special steps will be taken by all commanders to insure the strictest discipline and that all troops are in readiness and fully prepared to any eventualities. Division and brigade commanders and commanders of corps units will personally inspect all organizations with the foregoing in view.[8]

Less than an hour later, another "message" came from the Germans, one that killed four Ninetieth Division men. One man died in Mouzay only a half hour before the 11:00 a.m. armistice. The Yanks from a nearby division promptly answered back.

"The German artillery had a little spree before abandoning their guns. Mouzay was shelled about 8:30. The 155th Field Artillery Brigade (of the Eightieth Division) replied with retaliatory fire until 9:30 a.m., when all firing ceased," according to the division's history.

Three days later, Judge wrote a short letter home. He seemed almost apologetic for not writing sooner and showed signs of stress by misspelling more words than usual, including his girlfriend's name. His handwriting was shaky and his grammar had deteriorated. Once again, he wanted to assure his loved ones at home that he was all right.

> *Thursday, Nov. 14, 1918*
> *Dear Sis:*
> *I thot I would scribble a few lines to let you know I am*
> *Feeling fine and dandy at present and sure do hope that*
Ten
> *And Bill do also. I don't know were we are going now but the way things look it is going to be a place were we will be able to write at least once a week. We sure have been busy fighting for the last month. But have come out on top so we should not worry. Will write a fine long letter in a week and keep it up each week if possible. Tell John to not feel bad, that I don't write because I hav'nt been in a place to write for a month but will write every week from now on or no the reason why. Even Rubie did'nt get any of my spare time.*
> *Love to all,*
> *Judge*

Another letter soon followed, as promised. This letter was much more dramatic. In his own words, Judge described the intense battle on November 1, and the front on November 11.

Somewhere in France
Nov. 26, Tuesday
Dear Sis:
Well kid here it is two days before Thanksgiving and still no turkey in sight, but here is one boy that has something to be thankful for. The boys were torn to pieces all around me and I never got touch so I think that has turkey skinned all hollow, don't you? I will never forget Halloween night this year in all my life. We were waiting to go over the top the next morning at 3 o'clock and believe me we had the warmest reception I ever had in all my life. The Huns were figuring on making a counter attack the same morning, so we sure did go thru a strong barrack. The boys were falling all directions, but old Judge kept going. Well we got a little advance in no mans land when here came an old Hun carrying a white flag and had a bunch of his friends with him. They were afraid we were going to stick our bayonets in them. They kept on putting up there hands saying, comrade, comrade. Well we kept on capturing the huns the farther we went and we kept a going all day, so we sure did capture a bunch of them as well as killed them. We gain our objective the next morning and another battalion took up the advance. They had pretty good sailing after we starting the Huns on a run so they didn't lose many men. Our mail came that night with the grub. But it was some yelling going on for a while. The Huns got the news before we did because we could here them yell and holler worse than a bunch of wild Indians. It sure seems funny to be on the front and I hear no guns firing. I had to pinch myself a couple of times before I could realize the fact. Well old kid

I sure could sit down a write a book in no time, but I not going to at present. I spent over sixty days at the front and went over four times waiting for the fifth, which I am sure glad never came. I sure do hope and pray that Ten and Bill came out of the war as good as myself. Well tell the folks that I sure am hoping of being home before long to have a good cup of coffee and currant bread. Tell John I will sit down Sunday nites and tell him all about it, so he neednd worry about the old boy going back on him.
Love to all,
Judge

As for Bill, he did come out all right. Just before the armistice was reached, he wrote home on November 7, wanting news about Ten and Judge. By November 17, he is sleeping in a bed for the first time in a year at a hotel in southern France. He is enjoying the view of the snow-capped Alps, but hopes a peace treaty is signed soon. He wrote:

"It is a very nice place but give me the good old U.S.A. . . At this here place is where the American girls had better look out for their boys for most of the girls here fell for the American soldiers and say they are going back to the states with them and they sure mean it, but I doubt if they boys feel that way . . .

Judge recounted his experiences leading up to the armistice to Mildred.

"In the battle of the (Meuse-)Argonne, there were so many dead bodies you couldn't take a step without stepping on a body. So many were killed from Company G, 360th Infantry," Mildred said. "Judge said it was unbelievable that he went over the top so many times and was not wounded or killed. He had a guardian angel, for sure."

Once, Judge, marching single-file with fellow soldiers, came upon a dead German whose stiff arms stuck straight up in the air. Judge matter-of-factly approached the body, shook his hand and politely introduced himself. Everyone else following him did the same thing.[10] In ordinary circumstances this would be considered strange behavior, to say the least. During war, it was just something you did.

"At the end they were hungry, miserable with body lice. When they could, they turned their uniforms inside out and got relief until the lice crawled back in," Mildred said of the dismal conditions. They stole anything they could from the dead German bodies; they were so desperate for food, water and supplies.

"Daddy said he prayed a lot, but he was sure the young Germans were praying just as hard. Right before the armistice, there weren't many of them left. No one thought that they would make it home. One officer was left and told them he thought if they could make it one more night, the war would be over. Daddy said they dug foxholes with their hands and crawled in."

On the evening of November 10, Judge was most likely somewhere north of Dun-sur-Meuse and south of Mouzay, east of the Meuse River. The weather had turned bitterly cold. Judge and the Second Battalion were just behind the First Battalion, who was listed in the division's history as being along the northeastern edge of the Chenois woods, ready to lead the offensive at the designed hour. The Third Battalion was in reserve.

During the night, the two battalions had moved into position. Judge had braced himself to go over the top another time and kill more Germans. Even while he may not have been climbing out of a trench as there weren't many trenches in the area, it was the term he still used. Going over the top came to represent something more than the physical act to him. It became a mindset. He dug a hasty funk hole with his hands and tried to sleep until H-hour.

However, the morning of November 11, 1918 arrived, and Judge was shocked by what happened next.

"In the next morning they were awakened by cheering. The German soldiers came with straw in their arms for the American beds. Daddy said, 'These were the enemy – can you imagine?' They hugged and cheered together," Mildred said.

Apparently, Judge hadn't gotten the memo forbidding fraternization with the enemy or the "slightest relaxation of vigilance." Or, maybe he was actually informed that morning but just didn't care about rules from any memo. Ditto for the Germans who made the initial peaceful overture to Judge and his fellow surviving soldiers.

Not surprisingly, Judge's experiences on the morning of November 11 are not reflected in Wyeth's division history, nor the 360th Infantry history which stated the vigilance was not relaxed a moment that morning. When the Germans woke up Judge, they must have come earlier than the designated armistice time of eleven o-clock, possibly while it was still dark. Either that or the exhausted Judge fell asleep sometime after H-hour, which may have been possible since the infantry history states the offensive was held up after word was received about the armistice.

While violence continued along the front that day, even within his division, this was not the case for Judge. Maybe he just reacted to the day's events as a human being, not a soldier. He was no longer shooting Germans; he was hugging them.

Meanwhile, back home in Raymond, Minnesota, the hometown newspaper *The Raymond News* jumped the gun by reporting the war was over on Friday, November 8. So much for the accuracy of newspaper reporting in 1918, which was often the only source of news for some. The newspaper's deadline had to have been at least one day early, so they erroneously reported the end of the war four days early at best.

After the armistice was indeed reached, *The Raymond News* reported on the home front celebration the following week in its November 15 edition.

VILLAGE CELEBRATES VICTORY IN GRAND STYLE. ABDICATION OF EMPORER IS HAILED WITH DELIGHT.

Raymond joined the great national rejoicing at about noon on Monday. School was dismissed for the day at eleven a.m. and rapidly crowds began to swarm the streets. All buildings were flagged and the bells kept up a continuous ringing during the remainder of the day. The news had come that the armistice was signed and fighting would be stopped in a very short time. The Cornet Band furnished music during the afternoon and the jubilant crowd marched in procession throughout the entire village. Many a heart went out in profound thankfulness to the fighting American boys that had brought on the end of this terrible war.

While some newspapers had reported the end of the war before the fact, resulting in premature but understandable relief and celebration, in reality, the men were still fighting for their lives in Europe, especially Judge who faced dire conditions and was still in grave danger.

Then on November 11 itself, the decision by some to keep fighting for six hours after the armistice was signed earlier that morning at 5:00 is still fodder for debate among historians, especially since there were more casualties suffered on Armistice Day than on the D-Day invasion of Normandy on June 6, 1944.[11] The idea that Armistice Day could create so many casualties was a cruel ironic ending to a cruel war.

Once hostilities actually ceased, for the first time in a long while soldiers on the front line were now able to climb out of their funk holes and stand straight up like human beings . . . hear nothing but men talking, shouting, and singing, warm themselves by a fire, and have hope. In his own words, Judge wrote of the surreal quiet, having to pinch himself to process that it was real and not a fantasy.

By now, Judge had somehow undergone a tremendous transformation from being an inexperienced young man from Minnesota and green recruit to battle-tested warrior. Last year, Judge was pulling pranks in Raymond by tipping over outhouses on Hallow-een.[12] That very same night one year later, he was over 4,000 miles away preparing to go over the top in the midst of his most intense fight in the war, unsure if he'd ever come back.

Like many of the American doughboys, Judge was an ordinary man thrust into extraordinary circumstances. But he had, in fact, survived the most difficult and perilous part of the war. His faith, sense of humor, and luck helped him persevere. He told Mildred he also desperately desired to see his mother again, and that kept him going.

For Judge, the end of the fighting came with an unexpectedly kind gesture from the Germans.

View of the village of Bantheville, showing the results of heavy shelling, first by American artillery and later by the Germans

Photo from the *History of the 90th Division.*

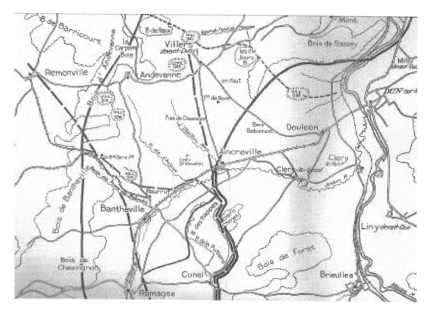

Meuse-Argonne map from *A History Of The 90th Division.*

Premature headline on the front page of the Raymond News,
Friday, November 8, 1918.

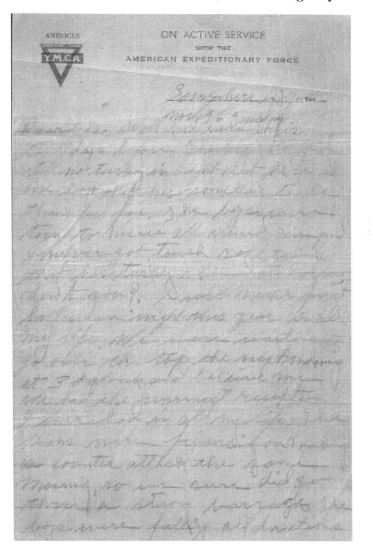

One of Judge's more dramatic letters written home on YMCA stationery November 26, 1918 from "somewhere in France."

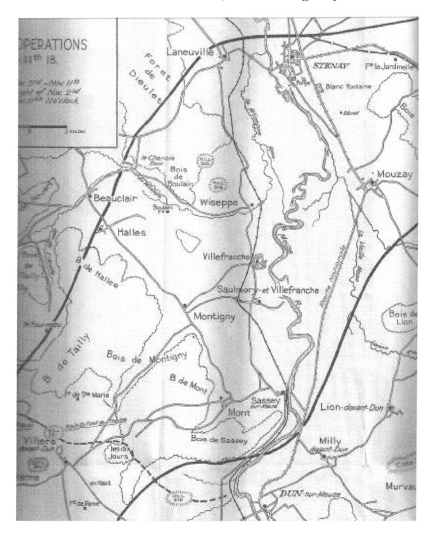

November 3-11, 1918 Meuse Argonne map from *A History Of The 90th Division.*

The Russians were rushin' the Prussians,
The Prussians were crushin' the Russians.
The good old Italians were hurling batallions
Canadians raidin' and Frenchmen invadin'
The Bulgars were bulgin' the Belgians
But Yanks started yankin' you see
And when Peace was conceded,
Some new maps were needed,
They ruined the geography.

The Russians Were Rushin' The Yanks Started Yankin',
1918 song by Carey Morgan

8 – Alamo Division Numbers And Notables

The Ninetieth Division never gave up a foot of ground in World War I.[1] The average advance in the St. Mihiel was three miles; in the Meuse-Argonne it was thirteen miles. They were under fire from August 20 to November 11, with the exception of seven days when they traveled between sectors.

The Division had a reputation within the AEF as being solid and dependable, consistently meeting its objectives. During their seventy-five days without relief, they took nearly 2,000 German prisoners--1,844 enlisted men and 82 officers.

According to post-war intelligence, the Ninetieth and Forty-second AEF Divisions were particularly feared by the Germans. This was revealed during US intelligence interviews with German officers after the armistice.[2]

The Ninetieth Division suffered the deaths of 1,042 men and 82 officers. Nine of those men were division buglers. Severely wounded were 1,257 men and 62 officers and slightly wounded were 4,671 men and 123 officers. Over 2,000 men and 81 officers were gassed.

Most of the men killed from Judge's Company G died from November 1-4, during the Meuse-Argonne. It was the greatest time of peril for him. Since the entire Texas Brigade on average was weakened in size to 65 percent for enlisted men during that time, the company could have easily slipped to around 120 men. Just within Company G, the casualties suffered during the Meuse-Argonne numbered a staggering 91 enlisted men, including those killed, wounded, missing, and gassed.[3]

The Ninetieth Division medical department held the record for the lowest mortality rate from gas, with only seventeen dying.

Also greatly aiding the doughboys in the Ninetieth Division were militarized representatives of three welfare societies: the Young Men's Christian Association (YMCA), Red Cross and Knights of Columbus.

The YMCA was the first welfare organization to join up with the division and stayed throughout the war. It offered canteens, religious activities, lectures, entertainment, reading and writing rooms, and hot chocolate free of charge during offensives. They were often just behind the front. Judge gratefully appreciated the services offered by the YMCA and wrote home on its letterhead stationery.

The Red Cross offered similar services including free candy, tobacco, newspapers, magazines, sweaters and other knitted items.

During the war, the various methods of communication between units included aeroplanes, runners and messengers, telephone, buzzer, ground telegraphy, radio, carrier pigeons, flares, rockets and projector lights. The telephone was the method most used by Field Signal units. To avoid German listening, the telephones stopped days before an offensive. The other methods were used somewhat, but infantry runners such as Judge were primarily relied upon in key moments.

"No mention of liaison would be complete without a tribute to the bravery of a group of men known as runners, who, when every other means had failed, were always ready to risk their lives to deliver a message for their commander. Within the battalion – from platoon to company, from company to battalion commander – where the fighting was fiercest, the runners had a monopoly on liaison; and further to the rear messengers were indispensable," Wythe wrote in the division history.

Code name for the Ninetieth Division was "Taylor"; for the Texas Brigade it was "Tuttle." The 360th code name was "Tide."[4]

Despite its accomplishments and reputation as a sturdy, reliable division that saw plenty of front-line action in the war, the Ninetieth rarely gets mentioned in history books.

Type of balloon observing for the 90th Division

Photo from the History of the 90th Division.

Our hearts today are far across the ocean,
God spare our boys, at night we kneel and pray,
In far off lands our troops are now in motion,
Among the very bravest in the fray,
For right and might must wipe out every wrong,
So let us hope it won't last long.

When the "Yanks" Come Marching Home, 1917
song by William Jerome

9 – Post-Armistice And The March To Germany

After the armistice, the 180th Brigade returned to the west bank of the Meuse River. Judge with the Second Battalion stayed one week at Villefranche. Surrendered German materials were collected. German prisoners were released.

The Germans, too, had released their prisoners of war. While Judge and his fellow doughboys were no doubt relieved when the armistice came, grim reminders of the war in human terms were all around them. At Stenay, Mousay, and Montmedy, the division arranged to feed Russian, French, British and American POWs, along with destitute French civilians wondering among the wreckage.

"Never were the hardships during the war more apparent than in the spectacle of these civilians carrying everything they possessed in little sacks on their backs, returning perhaps to find their homes completely demolished by shell fire," Wythe wrote in the division history. "Their expressions of joy for their deliverance by the Americans knew no bounds."

Judge soon learned he would not be going home any time soon. Instead, the Ninetieth Division had been chosen as one of nine combatant divisions to form the Army of Occupation of Germany.

Due to AEF concerns of the war reigniting, no one was going home soon. While an armistice had been reached, a peace treaty had not been signed. Even when the Treaty of Versailles seemed eminent, sufficient transportation was not available to quickly ship the doughboys home.

On a crisp Sunday morning on November 17 at 5:30, Judge began the trek into Germany. The Americans, along with the Belgian, French and British troops, began a methodical Allied march toward the Rhine River following withdrawing German forces.

Even though an armistice had transpired, the 360th Infantry took no chances. According to the regiment history, " . . . the war had not been definitely declared over . . . The German army was in full, and reported orderly, retreat two days ahead of the advancing Americans, but no opportunity was given for any enemy to catch the Crusaders unprepared. Gas masks were worn at the alert position every day of the march and full field equipment was carried, as well as the ordinary issue of ammunition for each piece."[1]

From November 24 through mid-December, Judge and his division marched about 130 miles through France and Luxembourg into Germany. They averaged fifteen miles a day wearing heavy accoutrements. The Ninetieth Division was now part of the Third Army, Seventh Corps of the AEF. Its course followed the Moselle River.

Smart appearance and marching form was stressed as the doughboys were on display. Elated French towns greeted the US troops with cheers as the Americans were the "deliverers." The Texas Brigade was in Marville from November 24 through 29; in Villerupt November 30 through December 2; and Aspelt on December 3.

In Luxembourg, they were in Remich from December 4 through 5. The people in Luxembourg, like the French, were overjoyed to see the doughboys. The contrast was stark between the devastation of France and the neutral Luxembourg. Just seeing young people in civilian clothes seemed strange.

As Judge and the troops neared Germany, the air of exuberance was replaced by indifference. Then on December 6, they set foot on German land. They found the roads immediately improved and were in excellent condition. On December 6 they entered Saarbourg; the seventh, it was Konz; the eighth was Schweich; the eighth and ninth was Wittlich; the eleventh through thirteenth was Alf; the fourteenth through twenty-first was in Daun; and December 22 was Wehlen.

Just after arriving in Germany, division billeting officers set out to find a bed for every man. Even privates, if not sleeping in a German bed, were furnished with a bunk and bed sack filled with clean straw.[2] A weary but relieved Judge wrote his sister about his long journey. Accustomed to flat Raymond, Minnesota, he is impressed with the scenery.

> *Brimm, Germany*
> *Dec. 13, Friday*
> *Dear Sis:*
> *Well the old boy sure is going some, eh. First France, and then we traveled thru Luxemburg and last Friday we stepped into Germany. It sure is a beautiful country. We have been traveling on foot with full hacks weighing close to one hundred lbs. The packs get rather heavy by the time we stop, but we know we are not going over the top so we keep on smiling in spite of sore and tired feet. We are headed for Coblenze, about a three days march from where we are located at present. We go about twenty-five kilo a day, and at night we sleep in some German's hay barn or house, just how lucky we are. Another kid and myself are writing on a table, in a room belonging to a schoolmarm. She is one of the prettiest girls I have ever met. She can talk French and Dutch, but nothing doing when it comes to*

English but we talk all the dutch we know and she talks all the English she knows, so between the three of us we get along. The German people treat us fine. I hope peace will soon be signed so we can sail for the good old U.S.A. before many more moons. So little Elroy has flat feet and got in the fourth class. That sure is some joke on the boy. Tell him to go easy on my pants because I might be back sometime this winter and will need them. It is'nt a bit cold here. It don't even freeze at present. Will write again before long.
Judge

Back in Minnesota, Judge's youngest brother Roy, teasingly called Elroy by Judge, was nineteen years old. September 12, 1918 had marked the first day of the third draft registration, now expanded to include men 18 to 45 years of age. The very first day he was eligible, Roy went to Willmar to sign up. Some time after Roy's registration, his father William supposedly marched into the local draft board in Willmar and demanded that Roy not be drafted as the war had taken away three of his four sons.[3]

In Judge's letter, he referenced Roy's flat feet, but whether Roy actually had such problematic feet to be exempted from the draft by the examining physician in Kandiyohi County will never truly be known. There was nothing listed under physical disability. His cousin Carlton's draft registration and examinations listed flat feet, but that did not stop him from being drafted and placed in the infantry, although Roy probably had no knowledge of this. Perhaps flat feet became a generic catch-all phrase Judge used to indicate some sort of deferment.

In World War I, there had been five draft classifications that were called up in numerical order except for the fifth classification, which was exempt from induction and reserved for federal officers, clergy, etc.[4] Local draft boards were guided by many factors in deciding whether men received deferments. Judge refers to his brother's flat feet, but Roy more likely received an agricultural or dependency deferment.

Roy Lester Knott was said to be upset and resented his father's actions, some thought for the rest of his life.[5] Perhaps Roy was afraid of being labeled a slacker, a pejorative term popular at the time for draft dodgers, shameful loafers, and those who did not do their part in the war. Roy married a woman named Sally in 1934 and had one child, Loren. Years later at a family reunion, Loren referred to his father as "the one who did not go to war."

"He wanted to go," he emphatically stated. "He was mad about it," he added about the deferment. Still, Loren said that Roy may have come to eventually understand his father's reasons. Loren had no idea about Roy's supposedly flat feet.

Map from the *History of the 90 Division*.

The 360th Infantry crossing into Germany at Remich, Luxemburg

Photo from the *History of the 90th Division.*

Keep the home fires burning,
While your hearts are yearning.
Though your lads are far away
They dream of home.
There's a silver lining
Through the dark clouds shining,
Turn the dark cloud inside out
Till the boys come home.

Keep The Homes Fires Burning, 1914 song
by Lena Guilbert Ford

10 – Living With The Germans

For nearly six months, Graach, Germany would become Judge's new home. It is located just north of Bernkastel-Kues in the Moselle River valley, a breathtakingly picturesque Germanic countryside surrounded by steep vineyards, medieval buildings and a thirteenth-century castle. Not that there was any doubt, but Judge was definitely not in Minnesota anymore.

The Ninetieth Division set up headquarters in Bernkastel at the Hotel Zur Burg.

The German people were indifferent but obedient to the American troops, according to the division history. The Army of Occupation's primary military activity was guarding bridges and stations along railways. While Germany had agreed to an armistice, a peace treaty had yet to be signed.

The first two months of occupation stressed training, maneuvers, parades, ceremonies and drills. About the last week in February activities shifted to athletics, entertainment and education. The Yanks could attend elementary school classes (some had not finished) or even high school algebra as part of the "university in khaki."

"Don't forget that it will take many months to bring back our army from France," wrote *The Raymond News* on November 15, 1918, in a front-page article on the United War Work Campaign. The campaign brought together seven organizations—the YMCA, YWCA, Knights of Columbus, Jewish Welfare Board, American Library Association, War Camp Community Service, and the Salvation Army—into one large fund-raising umbrella group.

"Plans for the work of these organizations during the period of demobilization were mapped out long before the prospect of peace was even as near as it is today. There will be a regular "university in khaki" in France, for one thing. Our fighters will be able to make profitable use of their leisure—to fit themselves for bigger things when they get back into civil life, for better jobs. They have learned to learn in the army and navy. Text books, lectures and class-rooms must be provided to help them prepare for advancement after they return. The county's greatest educators are in uniform now, ready for this work.

"When he gets through fighting, let's show him what we think of what he has done! Don't let anyone tell you that the work of these seven organizations will be over when the war is over . . .That's when he will need most the entertainment and diversion supplied by these organizations. That's when he will want movies and concerts and ballgames and track meets to keep up his spirits in the inevitable delay before he comes home."

During these months of waiting and adjusting, Judge was exposed to the German way of life with German civilians on German soil.

"After the war, Daddy lived with a German family as part of the occupation forces. I think this is where he saw a big chime clock and always wanted one. The Texans drilled for three hours in the morning and at three o'clock he went on guard duty," said his daughter Mildred.[1]

Judge wrote a letter to his sister Etta on Christmas Eve from his new home in Graach.

Tues. Dec. 24, 1918
Graach Germany
Dear Sis:
Well kid I bet you never expected to have a brother spend Xmas in Deutscheland, eh? The Captain told us last night to make ourselves to home because we might be in Graach the whole winter. Graach is a fine place located on the Mosel River and about forty kilo from Trier. He said we probably could get twenty-four hour passes to visit Trier. I have got a fine bedroom with a featherbed in it, so you see I won't get cold this winter. The weather sure is fine in this country. It has'nt froze here to amont to anything since I been here. The German people raised most all grapes here and lived mostly off wine. An old lady runs the house I am staying in at present and she can'nt see how it is I nix firstay.* I have to go thru the darn'st motions to get her to understand me. I bet it would be rather interesting to hear a conversation between the old lady and myself. First we all hoped to be home by Xmas but have change our minds since, probably will be next xmas. We have walk "with full hack" for twenty-three days, so you can imagine my poor little toes are blister right smart. I think Bill and Ten will be sent back home before long because they only have good fighters to settle up things in Germany. These people sure do treat the American soldiers fine, but they hav'nt got no time for the Frenchmen. The people don't want us to leave their homes after we stay there a few days. The girls generously kiss us good bye, "not so bad eh?" Well I wish you all a very Merry Xmas and a happy new year.
With love to all
From Judge
*unknown meaning

Another letter followed. Judge now had ample opportunity to write home. Coming down from the psychological and physical highs of battle, celebrations, and marching through Europe, he was showing signs of boredom and homesickness. He even misses the snowstorms in Minnesota. The overwhelming changes and rootless instability of the past months began to come through his writing. This letter was dated December 1, 1919. However, Judge probably meant January 1, 1919 as January 1 fell on a Wednesday (December 1, 1918 fell on a Sunday) and the letter fits in the chronology of events and places. It was his first letter written home in the new year.

> *Dec. 1* (Jan. 1?), *Wednesday 1919*
> *Graach, Germany*
> *Dear Sis:*
> *Well the old boy is still in Graach "on the Mosel River," and don't look much like getting home very soon either. We have been drilling five hours today, so we sure do get enough of that stuff, "eh." We get up at six-thirty and go to bed at seven so I believe we get plenty of sleep. It gets light here at about seven-thirty in the morning and gets dark at four o'clock sharp.*
> *What in the world is wrong with you Getchee, you never write anymore. I haven't received a letter from home for a month, so I don't know if you are all living or not, and it makes me feel blue once in awhile. I was on a wood detail yesterday and had a fine time sliding around the hills.*
> *Here it is Dec. 1* (Jan. 1), *and it hasn't frozen in Germany yet, so I am missing alot of old Minnesota snow storms. I got a letter from Rubie the other day telling me she had seen Carlton Knott's name on the C.* list. So I have been wondering if he is dead or not. The German people sure do treat us fine, alot better than the French people did.*

The girls think alot of the <u>brave</u> American soldiers and all want us to take them back to America with us. So don't be surprised if I come back with a nice young dutch** gal.

I was just wondering how Bill and his Grace are making it, and he still figures on getting married, as soon as he gets enuf money to pay the preacher. How is the Huisinga*** family now days, is everything running smooth and do they ever come to town? Is that flat footed bud of mine and yours making them chickens lay and the cows give alot of milk, or does he say let Judge do it?

There is a rumor going around now that we probably would go to Russia next, but golly I hope not because we would freeze in that cold country. I hope the next winter I see is dear old Raymond, Minnesota and the sooner the better. Will shut up for another week.

With love to all.

Judge

*casualty list

** Deutsch

**Raymond relatives

In a few weeks, Judge wrote Etta again, still homesick. Once again, he wondered about his brothers, and his dog Duke. Apparently someone else back home had caught the attention of his girlfriend Ruby.

Graach, Germany
Jan. 18, 1919
Dear Sis:
I received a letter from you the other day and I was sure glad to hear that everybody was fine. Well I am feeling pretty well myself today for having a bad cold. I have had a cold for the last two weeks, but it is getting better now. The weather sure is fine over here, it never freezes so we don't

wear gloves. The sun don't shine here very much, and it rains quite a bit so imagine that's the reason we have so many colds. I bet Jennie* is glad her Edward is back. I wish I was back also telling all about the affairs we had with the Huns. I haven't heard anything from my big brothers since I left home, so I don't know if they are in the Occupation Army or not. We had inspection this morning so won't have anything to do before Monday except formations. I guess I am going to get a pass to bern castle tomorrow and get my picture taken. If I do I will send a few along with my next letter, so you can take a look at the old boy. I have not heard from Ruby for a deuce of a long time, so probably she married by this time. I wished for an announcement, but such is life in the wooly far west, none came. I should worry there is still good fish in the sea that have never been caught. If you don't believe me "ask John." I get a little homesick once in awhile, but it don't last long. It would never do for a soldier to have the homesickness blues all the time, or he would spoil the little good time he has.

We see a real good show about once a week, "home talented." You know with so many boys there always is a few show actors as well as farmers. Say kid you never wrote and told me what Ben** was doing for a living these days, since he had an auction sale.

I bet it is about forty below zero in Minnesota at present, and a few feet of snow on the ground. Well I will miss one cold winter anyhow, even if I start back in a few weeks.

The German people are hauling manure up on the grape fields with a little basket, which fits on their backs. I get all in trying to walk up the hills, let along having a big load of manure on my back like the Germans do.

Well I hope to be back before many more months go by and see how the old states are coming. Will write again in

a few days. Hoping this letter find you all in the best of
health. I remain your <u>loving</u> brother.
Love to all even Duke
Judge
  *Judge's aunt
  **possibly Ben Miller or farmer Ben Mielker, both of Raymond

Three letters followed in February, including one sent on his
birthday, February 26. Judge had turned twenty-three years old
while living in Germany, where the flu pandemic had reached. He
fondly remembers the "sweet Texas girls" and does a little
boasting.

Graach, Germany
Feb. 9, Sun., 1919
Dear Sis:
    I received your and Grace's most welcome letters Fri-
day, so will endeavor to answer them right away so you
can see I enjoy them more than you imagine. It was over a
month that I didn't get a letter, so I thot the whole bunch
had done gone back on me. I am still in Graach living with
Grandma, so between me and the old lady we know each
pretty well. I go on guard at three o-clock this afternoon,
so will have to liven up from head to foot.
    I just came back from the Y where the chaplain held ser-
vices for an hour. It getting colder here every day now,
even the Mosel is freezing on the sides and it has also
started to snow, so I guess I will have a bad night of it on
guard. But it will all be over in twenty-four hours. We only
drill three hours in the morning now, so have the afternoon
off, "not so bad eh." I don't think it will be so very long be-
fore we start for the states. The people of Houston, Texas
are going to have a big blow out for the 360 when we get
there. The Texas boys get letters from their folks, telling

them about the wonderful time they're going to show us, when we get back. I suppose we will parade for them once a day, and the rest of the time to our selfs, so we ought to enjoy ourselfs the rest of the day with all them eats and the sweet Texas girls, eh. Wait till the 90 div. comes back or the combat troops, the girls and mother will have something to be proud of. I just busted all the buttons off from my blouse practicing how I was going to walk when I get back; but I think I might talk a little bit to common people when I get back probably it will be how do you do or good evening. I think that will be about all. Well it getting near dinner time so will shut up. Answer right away Jeannette and tell me all the news and tell Grace this is half hers so she should write to.
Love to all
Judge

Feb. 26, 1919
Graach, Germany
Dear Sister and all:
    This being my birthday I thot better as I write to let you all know how the old boy is navigating thousands miles from home in the service of his Uncle Sam. There is going to be lecture on the history of the Mosel River at the Y, so will have to hurry this letter along. I was surprised to hear in your last letter about John Feig being wounded and in the hospital. I had'nt heard anything about it before. I sure am glad to hear that all the boys in Raymond pulled thru O.K. It sure is remarkable. I thot sure my insurance was collectable for awhile on Nov. 1. The boys were falling on all sides of me and did'nt know but what I would be the next, but I sure am right there when it comes to keeping my carcass flat on mother earth. We have had a little trouble with a few smart Germans lately. One of them came over to

Graach to see his girl the other day and he started to make smart remarks about the American Soldiers and got put in the guard house. Another German who runs the wine shop sold wine after hours, and we had him picking up cigarette stubs for a week on the streets. An order came out the other day to let no two soldiers sleep in the same bed on account of the "Flu," I guess so all Germans in the military age has to turn over their beds to us, "not so bad eh." I bet Getshee you would have to be sleeping on the floor yourself if we had'nt won this war. Well it getting near time for that lecture so will shut up.
With Love to all
Judge
P.S. I thank you for telling me that my birthday is on the 26th of Feb., but please tell me in the next letter how old I am. Ha!

The last February letter is addressed to another sister Grace and mentions her boyfriend, Rich Portinga, and their cousin Albert Huisinga and the town of Svea, near Raymond, Minnesota.

Feb. 29, 1919*
Graach Germany
Dear Sis:
 I was thinking tonite about you being about the only sis I have neglecting since I went in the service of Uncle Sam. I have received several letters from you, but have'nt answer that many I know. I suppose you are rather lonesome out among that bunch of Dutchmen. I know it use to get my goat when old Portinga use to bawl me out for smoking. I suppose old Rich makes things a little lively for you, or has he another girl. How in the world is George and his frau making it? Do they ever have a family quarrel? I suppose Albert has to go out to Svea alone now or has he got mar-

ried ok? I have been playing basketball the last two weeks so have'nt stood no formations. It sure seem good to get out of drill for a while at least. The Moselle River sure has got high the last two days. It almost comes up to our house. We use to drill right beside the river, but now it is cover with water, so the drilling is done along the road. These German girls sure are a bunch of lunitics. They are hardly civilized. I sure am proud I belong to the good old U.S.A. Only one soldier is aloud to sleep in a bed now so I have the bed to myself now. We drew straws to see who got out, and I was the lucky guy. One of the boys in our squad got a discharge today, and started for the U.S.A. at eleven bells. He sure was a happy kid. He lives in Minnesota not very far from St. Cloud. Well it is getting about time for me to hit the hay so say hello to the Huisinga Bros for me and the Nelson sisters. Tell Aunt Jennie to be sure and have a big piece of pie for me when I get back because I sure will be out there.

With love
Your Boy Judge
Write right away
P.S. Tell Albert to write

*There was no twenty-ninth of February in 1919, Judge must have meant February 28.

In April, something big happened to break up the monotony and routine.

On April 24, 1919, the AEF's Commander-in-Chief General John J. Pershing came to Wengerohr, Germany to inspect the Ninetieth Division. [2] The 180th Texas Brigade passed in review. Pershing presented Brigadier General McAlexander with the Distinguished Service Medal and other men with Distinguished Service Crosses. The entire division, which was now made up of 928 officers and 19,847 enlisted men, assembled to hear the man who had lead them through the war. Judge was thrilled to march before General Pershing. By this time, Judge's service record reflected him earning a "VG" (Very Good) rating as an automatic rifleman under "military qualifications." He also had received his gold V-shaped war service chevron to wear on the lower left sleeve of his uniform. The gold chevrons indicated six months of overseas service.[3]

Two days later, Pershing wrote a letter to the Ninetieth Division, singing its praises.

" . . . in the St. Mihiel offensive . . it attacked the strong positions on the Hindenburg line immediately west of the Moselle River. In these operations it was entirely successful, mopping up the Bois-de-Rappes, . . . and advancing to a depth of 6 1/2 kilometers. . . In the tremendous attack of November 1 it continued its splendid record, piercing the Freya Stellung, crossing the Meuse and taking 14 villages in its very rapid advance. . . By November 10 the infantry had crossed the Meuse and the town of Mouzay was taken. The Division was pressing the enemy hard at the time of the signing of the armistice.

"As part of the 3rd Army the Division participated in the march into Germany and the subsequent occupation of enemy territory. I am pleased to mention the excellent conduct of men under these difficult circumstances as well as for their services in battle. They are a credit to the American people . . .Sincerely yours, (signed) John J. Pershing."

Judge mentions the upcoming Pershing visit in his next letter.

Graach, Germany
March 28, 1919
Dear Sis:
I haven't wrote for sometime so thot I had better scribble a few line tonite before going to bed. Everything is going on about the same in old Graach. We get up at six forty five and I drill a few hours and then in the afternoon we don't

do much unless we are unlucky enuf to get on a detail. We were told that General Pershing was going to inspect us in the early part of April, so all we are doing now days is washing our equipment. The stuff going around now is that we are going to start for the states sometime in May so the old boy is liable to be home to celebrate the fourth of July yet. I got an answer to my letter from Tom Brown about a week ago telling me he was going to start for the states in a few days and that he would stop in Raymond a few days, if he went that way. I wrote Ten a dandy long letter sometime ago and he sent me back a darn postal card. I sent him back a postal telling him I wanted a civil answer. He is back in France waiting to relieve a div. that soon starts for the states out of the occupation army so I think I will beat him home. I don't know what div. Bill is in so don't know if he is to going to relieve any of the occupation Army or not. Well it is getting bedtime and I am on K.P. tomorrow so will close this stuff. Goodnite.
Love to all
Judge

Another letter soon followed to Etta and wrote of his much-anticipated homecoming to Raymond. Judge's doughboy days were winding down.

Graach, Germany
April 2, 1919
Dear Sis:
    I received your long newspaper and Jeanette's letter yesterday so will answer it this afternoon before we are called out for hay. Yes it is hay day today and I hope it will be the last before we sail for the U.S.A. It is getting warmer here every day and I am getting more homesick every day. I sure feel sorry for Ten if his div. has to relieve a div. in the Army

of Occupation. It probably will be fall before he will sail. I think we will sail in about a month and a half.

You want to have a big cake bake for me because you know I missed all the holidays even my birthday I spend in Graach Germany. I suppose Bill will beat me home if he was to sail some time ago. Don't believe any of the stuff he put out, because he stay way back from the front lines and made roads. As fast as the Infantry chased the Huns out the Engineers came up and fixed the roads. Well we just got hay off. I received fifty eight Francs so will have a little to spend eh.

There is going to be a show at the Y.M.C.A. tonite I think a moving picture show. They have a truck outside of the Y which gives the power to run the machine. Tell Punk not be bashful about writing to me because if he don't he will wish he had when I get back. It is getting close to retreat time and I have to blacken my shoes and clean my gun so will discontinue.
Love to all
Judge

Judge loved lemon-filled white cake with seven-minute frosting. He could almost taste it.

Meanwhile, Judge's brother Bill had been in Coublanc, France since the war ended. Bill started out drilling every day to keep busy, but ended up playing plenty of basketball. He had time to write home, where the influenza epidemic had struck the Knott family, luckily without any fatalities.

February 2, 1919
Dearest Mother:
Had a card from Hank the other day and he said he has written a few letters but I didn't get any of them so they

must have gotten lost. Say I heard Papa had the flue. Is that right? Hope he is well now . . .
Your son Bill

"Uncle Sam's Advice On Flu: As Dangerous As Poison Gas Shells," read the headline from *The Raymond News* on October 25, 1918, when influenza had spread through Minnesota. Soon after on November 8, the newspaper reported that the epidemic had postponed the departures of the last of the area recruits, which were to have left on October 21.

There were widespread waves of closings during the influenza outbreaks. The Epworth League, a Methodist young adult group that met at the Knott home in Raymond, cancelled its monthly meetings from September through the remainder of 1918. Etta Knott was president.

Bill's letters continued. A bit behind the times, Bill finally catches on about Judge and Ruby, but by this time, the dalliance had run its course.

February 9, 1919
Dear Sister:
I suppose most of the boys in the camps at home are being discharged from army . . . .Tell Bud Miller that he can be lucky he didn't see any more of the war than he did, for that is one thing I want to forget. Judge's Division might of went thru a good bunch but not ours. The last I heard of him he was in Germany in the Third Army and I don't know when they will be going home not very soon I think . . . say before I forget what did Judge do before going to war, for every letter you write you tell me about Ruby. Did the kid make a hit with her?
I remain your brother Bill
with love to all

During the next few weeks, Bill's unit was busy repairing roads in France, and he wondered about what will happen when he gets home and the job he left as a mason.

> *February 21, 1919*
> *Dearest Mother:*
> *Well how is everything at home and in the little city, suppose there is plenty of work yet. I mean building work . . . will go back to my old job I think. But if work is short there I think will go out west farther and start for myself in the some small town . . .*
> *Your Son Bill*
> *Love to all*

> *March 9, 1919*
> *Dearest Mother:*
> *We were left behind for awhile to fix up the roads and to make little rocks out of big ones . . . homesick for the states but there are lots of boys who have been here very much longer than we have and it is only fair to let them go first . . .*
>
> *my love to all*
> *Bill*

> *March 26, 1919*
> *Dearest Mother:*
> *I sure hate to write anymore. The one aim I have now is to get back so I can talk instead of writing . . .*
> *Bill*

Judge Knott, unknown, Richard Peters, unknown
in Bernkastel, Germany January 19, 1919; family photo.

Photo from the *History of the 90th Division.*

The towns of Berncastel (on left) and Cues (on right) on the Moselle River. Headquarters
of the 90th Division was located at Berncastel

Photo from the *History of the 90th Division.*

Consolidated band of 250 pieces

Colonel Suge, 315th Engineers, and staff

Reviewing the 165th Field Artillery Brigade

Reviewing the Horse Transport

General John J. Pershing reviews the 90th Division at Wengerohr, Germany, April 24, 1919

Photos from the *History of the 90th Division.*

Judge in uniform, date unknown, family photo.

America, I love you,
You're like a sweetheart of mine,
From ocean to ocean,
For you my devotion, is touching each bound'ry line,
Just like a little baby
Climbing its mother's knee,
America, I love you,
And there's a hundred million other's like me.

America, I Love You, 1915 song by Edgar Leslie

11 – Home

Mother's Day, a relatively new national holiday, must have been filled with a sharp sense of anticipation and acute longing for Annie Knott back in Raymond, Minnesota. It was President Woodrow Wilson who had issued a proclamation establishing the first national Mother's Day holiday just five year's prior, on May 8, 1914, before the Great War began and the prospect of drafting and sending young American men to a war overseas was unimaginable for many in the United States.[1]

Annie Knott knew the war was over. She knew her three sons survived. And she knew she would see them. Soon . . . while the peonies were still in bloom in late-spring Raymond.

Just after the war had ended, *The Raymond News* reported greetings to the "Minnesota Lads Over There" from Minnesota Governor J. A. A. Burnquist.

"The people of Minnesota are proud of their boys at the front. I have yet to hear of a Minnesota boy in the expeditionary forces guilty of any disgraceful act, but the stories of heroism and sacrifice are so numerous that they become commonplace," the paper read on November 15, 1918.

"Tell the boys that whatever stories they may see in the newspapers about seditious utterances, about slackers of various kinds, about war profiteers, are exceptional cases and in no way represent the average American. These happenings are printed as news simply because they are exceptional. I am convinced that it is unfair to say that any class or race of people of any section of our country is disloyal. The instant and ungrudging responses which our people have given to all war demands is proof of this. They have subscribed to all three Liberty Loans, they have given more than asked . . ."

United War Work Campaign drives also made front-page news in Raymond since the war ended. *The Raymond News* liked to report donor names with their exact dollar contributions.

Judge was correct when he wrote he would sail in about a month and a half. Between May 17 and May 25, the Ninetieth Division left Wengerohr, Germany via railway. They were the fifth out of nine divisions to leave Germany. By the end of May, they sailed from their port of embarkation, St. Nazaire, France.

Monday, May 27, 1919 was Judge's last day in Europe. Once they left Germany, the Ninetieth Division ceased to function as a division. Judge's days of serving his country were coming to an end.

In his last letter sent from Germany, Judge, not surprisingly, wrote about his mother soon seeing her "hero," and his dog, Duke. The boasting had resumed. Judge inadvertently mentions his brother "Hank" (Ten) being an engineer, but he must have been caught up in his swaggering and meant Bill.

> *April 23, 1919*
> *Graach, Germany*
> *Dear Sis:*
> *Well sis by the time this reaches the Knott family I will be or expect to be out of Germany. We leave for Port in about twenty days so I expect I will be muster out by the 1ˢᵗ of*

June, "hurrah hurrah" for the chicken ranch. They wanted us to reinlist for another year but I suppose Mother wants to see her hero, and her hero also wants to see his mother as bad, so I think better as I come home, "eh." I feel sorry for Hank (Ten) *because I hear his div. has to stay over here some time yet. I have sure been lucky since I got in the army. I hav'nt been sick enuf to be marked quarters. I only went to the infirmary once and then he told me I had better report back to the company to drill. I suppose sis I had better be tapping on wood to make things safe for bragging. I suppose Bill is back in the states by this time and telling about the narrow escapes he had in the S.O.S.* (Services of Supply). *Hank div. probably would of made themselves as famous as the 90ᵗʰ if the armistice had'nt been signed so quick but the engineers use their back instead of their brains and bayonet, and never would be but a <u>labor</u> class of people without much honor. The weather is fine now days even the sun shines. I am sure full of freckles on account of these little overseas caps and hot sun. Tell the school marms* (his sisters) *to wait if they want to meet me. I am sorry to hear that Ed Pslind had the misfortune of being sick after getting muster out. It is almost a year since I left home but it don't seem that long. Duke probably will bite my leg off, not knowing who it is. Give my best regards to all my friends and enemies and tell them I will soon be back. I think I will have a few million copys written about the war so I won't have to tell about it to everybody I see.*
As ever
Judge
Love to all
George Knott
Co. G 360 Inf.
Amer.Ex. F.
Ad. soon will be Raymond, Minn

According to Mildred, the sea was awfully rough on Judge's trip home. "There were a lot of sick men. Judge didn't get sick, but he said he would be eating from his mess kit and then the kits would all slide down the table and you would have someone else's food.

"He was so thrilled to see the Statute of Liberty. That was the most beautiful sight he ever saw. It meant he was really home."[2]

Once division troops debarked in the United States, the majority were sent to the demobilization camps of Camp Bowie and Camp Travis, Texas; Camp Pike, Arkansas; and Camp Dodge in Iowa.

Judge sent a postcard, compliments of the Jewish Welfare Board once he arrived in Boston, Massachusetts at noon on June 7, 1919. The front read, "Hello – Just Got Back . . . Going to Camp Dodge." The postcard said he sailed on the vessel USS *Mongolia*, a 14,000 gross ton passenger-cargo steamship built in 1904 and used by the navy during the war.[3]

On it Judge wrote:

> *Hank is sailing right behind me. How is Duke?*
> *Dear Mother:*
> *Just arrived. Will soon be ready for a big feed at home.*
> *Love*
> *George Knott*

The doughboys on the *Mongolia*, unfortunately suffered a major delay in docking due to the battleship *New Jersey*, who was in line ahead of them. When the *Mongolia* finally sailed down the channel, a joyous cacophony of deafening whistles, cheers, and sirens rang out.[4]

Some of the organizations of the Ninetieth Division paraded in a number of Texas cities before reporting to the demobilization camps. At Camp Travis, the 360th Infantry reputedly had the most spectacular reception of the division.[5]

Eager to get home, Judge understandably skipped the homecoming celebrations down in Texas. Other than the clothes on his back, Judge left Camp Devens, Massachusetts carrying a barrack bag with undergarments and an overcoat. It was all he had as he began his return journey to Camp Dodge, Iowa where his expedition all began. He was officially discharged and on his way back to Minnesota on Saturday, June 14. On the left sleeve of his woolen army tunic, he now wore two gold service chevrons, a red honorable discharge chevron, and a red TO division shoulder patch. On his right sleeve was a round khaki-green infantry patch with crossed rifles.

Judge the doughboy was going home!

What happened when Judge set foot in Raymond is almost unbelievable, but true. When he left for war nearly fourteen months earlier, Judge walked with his dog Duke to the bank corner across the street from the train station. Judge told him to stay. According to Mildred, his sisters later informed Judge that everyday Duke would walk down to the bank corner and watch the trains come and go. At dark, Duke would go home.

"In the spring of 1919, Duke was getting old and not feeling good. The family was so concerned. He still dragged himself down to watch the trains," Mildred explained.

"When daddy came home no one knew he was coming. He got off the train and saw Duke by the bank corner. It was a chilly day and Duke was shaking. Daddy unbuttoned his army jacket and tucked Duke inside to get warm. Daddy said the dog kept looking at him with love. Half the way home he laid his head on daddy's chest and died."[6]

Safely home after the war, Judge found his brother Sgt. William (Bill) H. Knott was already back in Raymond, having gotten there about a month before.

Bill was overseas nearly a full year from May 19, 1918 to May 9, 1919; first going into action June 30, 1918 in the Toul sector with the 307th Engineers. Bill took part in the same offensives as Judge, the St. Mihiel and Meuse-Argonne. He was the first Knott brother to leave Raymond and the first to return. He was discharged from Camp Dodge on May 21, 1919.

On May 11, 1919, Bill wrote his last letter home from Camp Upton, New York. He was now a sergeant and eagerly waiting to go to Camp Dodge.

> *Dearest Mother and all:*
> *Sure was sick coming over only lost nine lbs in eleven days from sea sickness. Didn't feel it at all when I went to France, but we had a small boat and a rough sea to start with so most of the boys were sick and we sure did feed the fish for a few days. But that is all over now and we sure are glad of it and it does feel good to be back in the old U.S. Don't expect to hear from you again till I get home, and don't think I will write again . . .*
> *Your loving son Bill*

Oldest brother Pvt. Tennus (Ten) W. Knott came home about a week after Judge. It must have been quite the homecoming with the three Knott brothers together again.

Ten had served with Company D of the Fifty-third Infantry, Sixth Division. He had been overseas nearly one year as well, from July 6, 1918 to June 12, 1919.

Ten was listed as being severely wounded in *Kandiyohi County in the World War* written in 1928. While not wounded in combat, Ten, however, developed a bad infection on the side of his head that required him to be hospitalized for a period during the St. Mihiel battle.[7] With basic sanitation often nonexistent and the constant scratching from the merciless cooties, infections were not uncommon in the infantry. Without the treatment of antibiotics, which had not yet been developed, even a minor scrape could turn serious.

Ten went into action about September 20, 1918 in the Vosges sector, and later fought in the Meuse-Argonne battle. He was also discharged from service at Camp Dodge, on June 21, 1919. Ten was the last Knott brother to leave and the last to return home.

Family members describe Ten as a dependable, quiet person who worked hard and stayed home. He spoke very little about his experiences in the war.[8] All of his war letters have vanished.

Judge received two medals after the war. Unfortunately, they became play toys of his first grandson and were lost. They included the Victory Medal with three clasps (Defensive, St. Mihiel, Meuse-Argonne), and the Army of Occupation of Germany Medal with the likeness of General Pershing on the front. The occupation medal was awarded to him on September 10, 1947, nearly thirty years later. The medals were reissued by the US Government by request of Judge's family in 2006.

Coming home and adapting to a civilian life had its challenges for the doughboys. Judge did not display any shell shock (now called post traumatic stress disorder) in his transition from front line to home front, but he was one of the fortunate ones. Mildred said Judge told her many soldiers "went 'beserk' from all the killing. There was no counseling–they were told to just suck it up and get on with their lives. His therapy was to talk about it, so it didn't fester inside. I was amazed by all the inner strength he always showed."

One thing always bothered Judge. Prayer had sustained him through the toughest of times. However, he also believed his opponents had prayed just as sincerely as he had, but those prayers had not been answered with the outcome they desired. It was an inner conflict Judge sought to reconcile for the rest of his life.[9]

Son-in-law Dennis Zetah, who had complained to Judge about the army in 1963, was also amazed at Judge's demeanor. Some soldiers, Dennis said, "would actually crack to the point where they couldn't function." With Judge, he never saw any remnants of shell shock or lingering disorders. "The guy was so stable. He was so in control. He knew what his job was. He thought the war was necessary, he knew why he was there. The things he saw and the things that he went through . . .

"Religion gave him direction in his life. That arrow was pointed straight north on his compass. He was on the path all the time," Dennis said.[10]

All three Knott brothers returned home. Their mother Annie must have been beside herself with joy.

But, not all parents had a happy ending.

Homecoming in San Antonio, Texas on June 17, 1919 featuring the 360th Infantry Regiment, Company A; photo from *A History Of The Activities And Operations Of The 360th United States Infantry Regiment In The World War, 1914-1919.*

This is more likely what greeted Judge after getting off the
train in Raymond, Minnesota, family postcard c 1920s.

Into a ward of the whitewashed walls
Where the dead and the dying lay-
Wounded by bayonets, shells, and balls-
Somebody's darling was borne one day.
Somebody's darling! so young and so brave,
Wearing still on his pale, sweet face-
Soon to be hid by the dust of the grave-
The lingering light of his boyhood's grace.

Somebody's Darling, poem by Marie Ravenal de Lacoste

12 – Carlton Knott And The Lost Battalion

Judge's aunt Bertha Knott Phiefer was one of those mothers who would have to live with the shattering news that her son was gone from this world. Five weeks before the armistice, Judge's cousin Pvt. Carlton V. Knott was killed in the war. Casualty Cablegram number 296 delivered the blow to his mother. Fortunately, Carlton's older brother Ray made it home okay.

Sgt. Raymond W. Knott was just about to enter the conflict at the front as an aerial gunner when the war ended. Ray wrote a long letter home to his mother Bertha Knott in November 1918, just after the armistice, and just about the time his mother received the devastating news of Carlton's death. Ray described the unbridled euphoria in France on November 11, but personally expressed mixed feelings about the war ending before he was able to leave his desk job and join the active fighting. While Ray wrote of his ambivalence, Bertha must have been massively relieved to hear from Ray and that he had not entered combat after all. The clock had run out.

Clearly, Ray had not heard the sad news about his brother Carlton, who had just been killed a few weeks earlier. In his letter, he refers to Carlton as "Kid."

Office of the Chief of Air Service,
Chaumont, France, Nov. 20, 1918
Dear Mother:

Some time ago I promised to write you a long, old fashioned letter . . . We were going ahead without a thought of peace, or at any rate all plans were being laid and work being done on the presumption that the war would continue forever. That was on November 10th. We were speeding right on ahead. Then all at once, at 11 o'clock the gear was shifted and we found ourselves headed straight back to the shores of Uncle Sam . . . I know that in me there was a complete reversal of everything. I had put in my application for Aerial Gunnery and it has gone thru all o.k. My plans of course were all laid up in the air and my one hope was that I should soon be called. In fact I received notice from the training section that I was of the next bunch to be called up . . .If I were the only one concerned I would say that six months more of this war would have suited me just right, but I know that there are many millions of others who are mighty glad it is over, and so I am glad, too. I have never been in the hard part of it, I guess that is why I wasn't so sick of it. I know all right what a bomb sounds like, and I've sat on the edge of a trench waiting for a piece of shrapnel to find me, but you know the boys in the infantry have not only that to contend with, but they have to live under conditions much harder than we of the Air Service do. Another reason I am bouncing with joy these days is Kid. He is in the infantry, and I know that he has and is doing much more of the work that a soldier is supposed to do than I have and am.

I suppose it was a glad day in the States when the news arrived. It was more than that here. It was almost an insane day. The evenings of the 11th, 12th and 13th were the wildest thing in the way of joy let loose and happiness unrestrained that I ever expect or hope to see . . . The streets were a mass of people all singing and cheering. I climbed up on the steps of the Hotel d'Ville, which is the Town Hall in French, and from there I could look down on all that took place. The sight there of those thousands of people swarming about in the half-dark singing and shouting, with the flags flying and the drums and bugles, is something that I for one will never forget.

I haven't heard from Kid. I suppose he has been moving about so that he didn't get my last couple letters. I am hoping every day to hear from him again so that I can tell if it will be possible to see him. I think probably that he will be on the army of occupation which is going up into Germany and if he is I'm pretty sure of beating him home . . .

Well, this has grown into a fairly good sized letter after all, and so I have fulfilled my promise. I will have many things to say when I see you but I can't seem to get them on paper. I only hope that Kid and I will be able to show up at the family board at the same time. After a year of "Corned Willie" etc., we sure will be able to appreciate a little sauer-kraut or bread with real butter on it. I suppose it is against the rules to hoard anything. If you can, though, try to fill the cellar up with pies and cakes etc., so that we will not run short the first day at least. Figure on about forty or fifty pies a day for each of us for the first week. After that we may get used to it and be able to eat more.

Au revoir ma cherie,

Your son, Ray

Sgt. R.W. Knott

Air Service,

General Headquarters,
American E.F.

Ray's younger brother Carlton was killed in action at the age of twenty-four on Friday, October 4, 1918 in the Battle of the Meuse-Argonne.[1] Carlton wrote his mother just a few weeks before he died. He asked about his brother and his Knott cousins. He assures his mother that he is in fine shape, learning some French, and eating blackberries.

In France
September 1,1918
Co. G, 158 Infantry
A.E.F.
Dearest Mother Mine:

How is Mother? I hope you are as well off as I am, for I'm getting fatter and lazier every day and I sure am feeling fine. This climate has everything beat I ever heard of. Just like a man would order it, to live, eat and sleep and grow fat.

I was out and had a bill of wild black berries yesterday and am going again today as it is Sunday and that means liberty day.

I am trying to learn French, but it is some talk, all I can say is "Good Morning and Good Night." And a couple more little things like that.

I haven't heard from Ray yet, in fact I haven't heard from any one for a month and for all I know there may not be any U.S.A. A person would think by the looks here that the U.S.A. has moved over here, Ha Ha.

If you know where uncle Wills boys are, let me know the Co. and Regiment they are in. I may be able to find them, but I can't find out a thing about where Ray is, no more than when I was there.

They are threshing around here now. Some threshing rig too. The old hand feed and they put it in careful, heads first and all the heads on one side so the straw doesn't get broken up so much. It comes out just about the way it goes in, only the grain is all out of it.

Well Mother mine, don't worry about me. I'm O.K. and couldn't be better off anywhere. Tell Sis (Pearl I mean) to write or I won't own her as a sister any more and--won't like her anymore, Ha Ha. Well bye, bye.
With love from your son,
Carlton

After he wrote the letter, Carton was transferred to Company B of the 308th Infantry, Seventy-seventh Division at the end of September. It was an unlucky transfer in retrospect.

Carlton had been with the Fortieth Division, which became the Sixth Depot Division once in France, supplying fresh troops to more experienced combat divisions.

Once in his new division, Carlton unfortunately become one of the roughly 679 men of the Lost Battalion, which was named to nine companies who became isolated in an Argonne Forest "pocket" during the battle of the Meuse-Argonne (accounts vary on the number of men who entered the "pocket" from approximately 550 to 679 depending on the source).[2] The men were under siege by the Germans for five days, from October 2 through October 7, 1918. Technically, they were neither lost nor a battalion. They were, however, famous soon after, if only for a short period of time.

The Lost Battalion received heavy publicity in US newspapers and within the AEF. Carlton's family undoubtedly soon became aware of the circumstances in which he died. Historians compared the valor of the surrounded men to that displayed at the legendary battles of the Alamo and Little Big Horn.[3]

The Lost Battalion became an icon of the war, symbolizing courage and defiance . . .no matter what the odds or how dim the prospect of victory seemed.

Carlton joined the Seventy-seventh Division along with a large number of replacements on September 23, just days before the attack.[4] He left New York on August 8, landed in England on August 16, and was in France soon after before he was plunked down onto the front lines with a new division in the largest US Army battle in history. If Judge's pre-combat training in Texas could be characterized as hasty and inadequate, Carlton's slapdash preparation was practically non-existent. Carlton was as green a replacement as there could be.

Some of the replacements had been in France less than a month, others had been in the service about that long and had spent that short amount of time in travel. Not only did many of the replacements have no reserve rations, there was no way for them to acquire any additional food or water. Some of these ill-prepared men jumped off into the Argonne battle and did not know how to work the magazines of their rifles, their hand grenades, and newly-issued bomb contraptions.[5]

According to a Lost Battalion summary at the National Archives called *The Operation Of The So-Called 'Lost Battalion'* written in 1928 by the Army War College, Carlton and the rest of his brothers in arms faced dire conditions. "Suffering extreme hardships from exposure, lack of food, water, and medical attention, this force repulsed incessant attacks of the enemy for five days and four nights."[6]

The situation was frightfully desperate. The wounded men lay bleeding and moaning in pain with no medical treatment. The unburied dead bodies of fellow soldiers lay all around, adding to the horror. There was nothing to eat and no water to drink.

All the while, they were blasted by the Germans. They were sitting ducks if they dared rise up from their funkholes. Surrounded and trapped, there was no escape.

Carlton's last few days were hell on earth.

One historian Robert H. Ferrell described the situation involving the stench of dead bodies.

"Beginning on Friday, October 4, it was impossible to bury the dead, whether the German bodies around the periphery of the pocket or, of more concern, the American ones within. The men were too tired. The ground in the pocket was hard to dig in, and space was running out, there being little between the trees or under bushes with frequently deep roots. In an unchivalrous act the Germans directed trench mortar, machine-gun, and rifle fire at burial parties," Ferrell wrote in his book, *Five Days In October: The Lost Battalion Of World War I.*

"There was a morale problem in leaving bodies aboveground, even if men covered the heads of the unfortunates . . . complicated by what be described as a smell problem, for the unburied made their presence known."[7]

In addition to repeated German attacks from all sides, they were tragically subjected to friendly artillery fire on Friday, October 4, the day Carlton was killed.

Carrier pigeons played a key communication role. One pigeon named Cher Ami was awarded France's Croix de Guerre Medal for his heroic actions. He delivered a message on October 4 from the Lost Battalion that read,

WE ARE ALONG THE ROAD PARALLEL 276.4. OUR ARTILLERY IS DROPPING A BARRAGE DIRECTLY ON US. FOR HEAVENS SAKE STOP IT.

Cher Ami made it back to his loft with the correspondence, but he had been severely wounded by the Germans. Even though he had been shot through the breast and blinded in one eye, he still delivered the message capsule dangling from ligaments of his leg that had been shattered. Army medics saved his life and he returned to the United States. Today, Che Ami's stuffed body is displayed at the Smithsonian Institute in Washington, D.C.

After five days of torment, the survivors of the Lost Battalion were finally rescued by US troops. It suffered a staggering rate of men killed, wounded, and missing. The morning of October 8 was described in the *History of the Seventy Seventh Division* written in 1919, "The 252 survivors of the 679 that had entered the 'pocket,' with their sick and wounded, marched south through the deep ravine to rest.

"Their hillside is now quiet. The dead lie sleeping in a little enclosure near the western border of the valley. The crash of minenwerfers and the whine of the bullets is stilled. But if the trees on this torn slope of France could ever break the silence, they would say 'By these splintered wounds you see upon us, we will live to mark the valor of the Americans.'"[8]

According to historian Ferrell, the Lost Battalion's important contribution was not what it represented or accomplished in the Meuse-Argonne battle per se.

"The story of the Lost Battalion kept alive the idea of courage," he wrote, "which became especially important for national morale in the 1920s, '30s, and the time after the attack on Pearl Harbor . . . courage almost was lost in a national revulsion against war in any form, as the notion became more widespread that war was fundamentally wrong.

"The division furnished one of the classic examples of courage, of what that priceless quality could bring out in the behavior of a group of apparently very ordinary Americans."[9]

Carlton was one of those ordinary men who did not walk out of the Argonne.

A headline from the Willmar Tribune in Minnesota read, "Carlton

Knott Sleeps In Hero's Grave In Poppy Fields of France" on November 27, 1918. The headline refers to a well-known poem written about the war called *In Flanders Fields* by Canadian John McCrae, even though Carlton died no where near the area known as Flanders fields.

In Flanders fields the poppies blow
Between the crosses, row on row,
That marks our place; and in the sky
The larks, still bravely singing, fly
Scarce heard amid the guns below.

We are the Dead. Short days ago
We lived, felt dawn, saw sunset glow,
Loved and were loved, and now we lie
In Flanders fields.

Take up our quarrel with the foe:
To you from failing hands we throw
The torch; be yours to hold it high.
If ye break faith with us who die
We shall not sleep, though poppies grow
In Flanders fields.

The obituary read, "He sailed to France in September and went to the front just before the last victorious battles and advance of our troops and was in the thickest of the fight. But, it was not to be his fate to return him with the other boys. But, he is now put in the poppy fields of France, with other heroes who gave their lives to rid the world of autocracy."

By that time, it mostly likely wasn't "news" in Raymond, Minnesota. To say the word of Carlton's death spread fast in the small town would probably be an understatement. Ruby Wagner, Judge's girlfriend, was the one that broke the news to him about Carlton being listed on the casualty list in a letter while he was in Germany with the Army of Occupation.

Judge's brother Bill had heard about Carlton from a letter from family friend Isabel Ryder. "Bet it was hard on aunty," he wrote in a February 2, 1919 letter from France to his mother.

During World War I, families began the practice of hanging service banners, although the banners were not standardized until World War II. Blue stars represented immediate family members serving in the war; gold stars represented ones who had died while serving.

On May 28, 1918, President Wilson approved a suggestion from the Women's Committee of the Council of National Defenses for American women to wear a black armband with a gold star, rather than donning the conventional black clothing signifying mourning. Whether the Knotts partook in these new practices is not known. American Gold Star Mothers organized in 1928, although Bertha never joined the new group that offered comfort to mothers who'd lost a son in the war, and loving care to hospitalized veterans confined in government hospitals away from home.[10]

According to Carlton's burial case file in the National Archives in St. Louis, Missouri, he was gunned down by a German machine gun. A fellow doughboy from his company, Pvt. Thomas Harries is listed as the informant.[11] His Immediate Report of Death form was completed and signed by Captain G. C. Graham of the 308th Infantry.

Carlton and the others who died in the "pocket" were buried by a detachment of the Fifty-third Pioneer Infantry. According to a book written twenty years after the war called, *The Lost Battalion* by Thomas Johnson and Fletcher Pratt, the burial detachment removed the two identification (dog) tags from each body; one was sent home with any identifying personal articles, the other they fastened to wooden crosses which bore the name of most of the men buried.[12]

Carlton was buried Sunday, October 13, 1918 in the American Cemetery in the Argonne Forest near Binarville, France, a town near the "pocket" where Carlton died nine days earlier.[13]

Once Carlton's brother Ray received news of his brother's death, he was determined to find his grave. The last time Ray and Carlton had seen each other was back in Great Falls, Montana in the summer of 1917 when they had filled out their war registration cards on the same day and Ray enlisted two months later.

In late winter 1919 while he was still in France, Ray set out to reunite with his little brother. In March, he wrote his sister describing the details of his emotional and difficult journey.[14]

Chaumont, France
Mar. 13, 1919

Dear Stranger Sis:
Your letter of Feb. 22 arrived today. I think I answered your last letter but wouldn't swear to it.

We are going on here very much the same. A little more work is coming thru. We are to write a book on liaison between Infantry and Air Service. That ought not to take more than two weeks and maybe then we can come home. I surely thought last month that we would be on the way by this time. But now I wouldn't be at all surprised if we were kept here until well along in April.

Right after payday, I went up to visit Kid's grave. It was a long and hard road and took three days. Got up to Verdun all OK. There I fell in with an engineer who was up from the coast to see the old battle grounds. I invited him to go with me. We went by train to a little town called Aubreville, but there really is no town there anymore. From there we had to hike. We spent our first night at Varennes where a company of engineers are stationed and next morning we struck out in the Argonne. We wandered about in the woods all day in the rain. About sundown I climbed up into an old German observation tower and from there located a solitary building on the far side of the woods. We went to it and found that it was the only building standing of the whole town of Binarville. We slept there that night and next day struck out on the road to Apremont. About a mile out we passed thru the German dug-out town of Charlevaux and a little beyond that, down in the bottom of the valley is the Moulin de Charlevaux (Charlevaux Mill). It is only a ruin of a mill but what there is of it stands beside a creek that just there falls over a dam. The hills on either side are high & rough & covered with woods but the bottom of the valley even at this season is green and level gently sloping down to the stream that runs down the middle of it. On the left side of the stream just where the trees end and the meadows begin is a long double row of wooden crosses with one big cross surmounting them all. The chaplain had written to me that Kid's grave was number 75, so I went to No. 75 and found it was marked "Unknown, Harry Miller." It was awful, sis, to think the Kid had died unknown even to his pals, but while I was kneeling there staring at that "Unknown" the chap that was with me called me over to number 38. There was a tin plate fastened to the cross on which was stamped "Carlton V. Knott, Co. B 308th Inf. Killed Oct. 4, 1918" and below it was nailed the identification tag he carried around his neck. It was our buddy, sis. When I left him in Great Falls all married & apparently happy, I little thought that I would soon be standing by his grave away out in the Argonne Woods. There was nothing to do. I dug up a flower from the woods nearby and planted it on his grave. Then we started the long hike back to the railroad. I didn't take a picture of the grave as mother wished me to do because I couldn't get hold of a camera. But his regiment will undoubtedly have some taken and we can get one from the address I sent mother.

I'm getting anxious myself to be home again, and I want too to get to know you all once more as you are and not *just as you were ten years ago. It is almost unbelievable but it is just eleven years ago that I went to N. Dak. to teach school and since that time I have been home only once. That was in the spring of 1914 when Kid and I came together and that is five years ago. According to that I must be getting older, tho, frankly I don't seem to be. I'm afraid I won't be able to stay long this time either, as there are so many things to do and life is so short. I had made plans to settle down when I got back. In fact I had a beautifully schemed castle all complete in the air which I intended to bring to earth this summer, <u>but</u>?*

At any rate, sis, I'll stay long enough to talk a lot and let you get an idea of the manner of person your Brother is. I hope it will be soon. Until then, Goodbye.
Your Bro,
Ray
Sgt. R.W. Knott
Hqrs Flight Air Service
GH2 AEF

Ray wrote of a grave that read "unknown." There were so many unknown graves of AEF soldiers in France that one representative unidentified body was shipped to the United States and buried in Arlington, Virginia at Arlington National Cemetery. It was called the Tomb Of the Unknown Soldier or Tomb of the Unknowns, and dedicated in a formal ceremony on November 11, 1921.[15] General Pershing attended the event. Also present was famous doughboy Sgt. Alvin York, and the leader of the Lost Battalion, Major Charles Whittlesey. It was the last public appearance of Maj. Whittlesey as he was presumed to have committed suicide by throwing himself off a ship within days of the dedication.[16]

By July 1919, Ray Knott was safely back home in Great Falls, Montana, after being discharged with a $60 bonus from Fort D.A. Russell in Wyoming. Seeing his loved ones again must have been intensely emotional for Ray, and Ray's reunion with his mother Bertha must have been extraordinarily overwhelming for both of them.

The following year, Ray wrote the war department looking for a photograph of his brother's grave. His mother had also requested a photograph, which were made available to the deceased families upon request.

> *415 3rd St.*
> *Great Falls, Mont.*
> *Aug. 9, 1920*
> *Sirs:*
> *Was there ever a picture taken of the little cemetery in the Argonne Forest near the Moulin de Charlevaux about 4 or 5 kilometers N.E. of Binarville where the dead of the so-called Lost Battalion of the 77th Division were buried? My brother Carlton V. Knott Co. B, 308th Infantry was buried there and I would like to obtain a photograph of the place if possible to do so.*
> *Thanking you I am.*
> *R W Knott*

That same year, Ray Knott made good on his plans to settle down and married Alice Phiefer, the daughter of John Phiefer, who married his mother in 1907. Alice was technically his stepsister but no blood relation.

In July 1919, Bertha Knott received Carlton's personal effects including a gold pocket watch and chain, and a memo book. As for Carlton's body, it ended up being moved several times before finding its final resting place.

On March 28, 1919, six months after Carlton's initial burial and soon after Ray visited the "pocket," Carlton was disinterred and reburied in grave number 111 at the Battle Area Cemetery in Romagne, France. According to Carlton's burial case file, one identification tag was found on his body at his initial disinterment, the other was fixed to a cross marking his grave just as Ray had described in his letter.

The file stated Carlton, upon disinterment, was still in his uniform. The body was noted as badly decomposed and wrapped in burlap. He was measured at 5 feet 10 inches tall, with an estimated weight of 174 pounds. His hair is listed as straight and light brown.[17]

Carlton's mother Bertha was listed as next of kin. He is noted as unmarried without children. There was no mention of any dependent child, which was listed by Carlton in his 1917 draft registration.

Carlton's file did include an emergency address of Mrs. Daisy Helen McCallum of 323 Wallace Avenue in Coeur d'Elene, Idaho. What her relationship was to Carlton is unknown, although Carlton had the same Wallace Avenue address listed as his residence just before he was drafted so they may have been fellow boarders. No wedding or divorce record of Carlton's has been found; nor has there been any trace of a child. Perhaps the child died or was a stepchild of his former wife.

Nevertheless, in November 1920 after Carlton's mother had moved out west to Washington State, Bertha Knott Phiefer wrote the war department to tell them she wanted her boy home.

> *November 15, 1920*
> *Mrs. Bertha D Phiefer, Clear Lake Washington*
> *Washington War Department*
> *The adjutant General office Washington*
> *Dear Sir:*
> *I noted that some of our boys are being sent home, and that stirs up the hope again of my boy too coming home. So I thot I would write you as to my address. We have sold out in Minnesota and have settled here and as I filled the application to have Carlton sent to Raymond, Minn. I would*

ask if it is possible to have him shipped here. he was reburied. his name Carlton V Knott Private 308, Co. B, 77 Division Argonne American Section #5, Plot#3, Romagne-Souse-Montfaucon, Meuse, France, was killed Oct. 4, 1918. Will you kindly let me know weather or not I can get my boy. he was my son by my first husband now dead for 25 years. I would like to have my son sent here to this place.
Mrs. Bertha D Phiefer
Clear Lake Washington
P.S. this is on the northern Pacific Rail Road.

Just over two years after being killed, Carlton was once again disinterred on May 24, 1921.[18] His body was embalmed and placed in a casket to ship home from France to Hoboken, New Jersey, Carlton's port of embarkation as a fresh recruit three years earlier. Carlton's remains, along with the remains of forty-three other doughboys ranging from privates to corporals and one cook, traveled on the Northern Pacific Railroad, escorted by US Captain John F. Gleaves.[19]

On July 24, 1921, Carlton came home.

He lies in a grave in Clear Lake, Skagit, Washington. His mother and stepfather's graves are nearby.

Along with others of the then-famous Lost Battalion, Carlton was once a symbol of courage. Today, sadly, he has been largely forgotten. Even within his own Knott relations, Carlton became only vaguely recollected by some in the very next generation.[20]

Ray Knott's granddaughter Candice Knott Holloway said her grandfather passed away when she was 12. "I don't have any personal knowledge of Carlton. I spoke with my brother Russell and he doesn't recall hearing grandpa saying anything about Carlton. Of course he was 15 when he passed, so might not have been tuned in to adult conversations. I know my father never spoke of him.

"You know these 'old guys' never liked to speak of painful memories, so I doubt he ever really talked about him. Unfortunately, now my brother and I are the 'old guys' in our family, so those memories are forever lost. It's really sad, because I love history," she said.

Whatever happened to Carlton's ex-wife and dependent child remains a mystery to this day.

In 2008, ninety years after the Meuse-Argonne battle, a Lost Battalion monument was unveiled in Binarville, France, the small town near the "pocket." The formal unveiling ceremony included a release of pigeons.

Sgt. Ray W. Knott c. 1919, family photo courtesy of
Candice Knott Holloway.

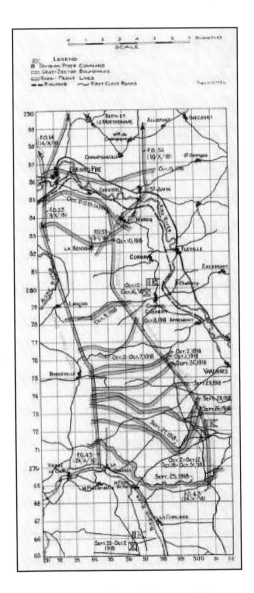

Argonne map from History Of
The Seventy Seventh Division.

The "pocket" photographs from *History Of The Seventy Seventh Division.*

Lost Battalion monument, Binarville, France, 2008;
photo courtesy of Dutch US Doughboys.

Lost Battalion marker, Binarville, France, 2008;
photo courtesy of Dutch US Doughboys.

Carlton Knott's gravestone (note his first name is misspelled and there is no denotation of Carlton being a member of the Lost Battalion), Clear Lake, Washington; family photo courtesy of Gayel Knott.

A Lion met a Tiger as they drank beside the pool;
The Tiger said: "Pray tell me why you're roaring like a fool."
"That's not foolish," said the Lion with a twinkle in his eyes;
"You see, they call me 'king of the beasts' because I advertise."
A rabbit heard them talking, and he ran home like a streak;
He thought he'd try the Lion's plan;
His roar was just a squeak.
A fox came to investigate – had luncheon in the woods;
So, when you start to advertise,
Be sure you've got the goods!

poem hung in Judge's shop, author unknown

13 - A Tough 'Ombre To The End

Upon his return home, Judge found his girlfriend Ruby had married someone else, just as he suspected.

In the fall of 1920 with the money he saved during the war, Judge purchased a shoe and horse harness repair business near the bank corner in Raymond. The frugal Judge had saved nearly all his money, not squandering it on French girls in Paris, which was something he accused his brother Bill of doing. The twenty dollars a month he received during the war had added up.

The harness shop was next to the meat market known for its home-made bologna. The meat market was owned by an industrious German family by the name of Wegner.

One day as he was walking by the meat market, an attractive young lady in the window caught his eye. He stuck his head in the doorway and said hello. He learned the lady, named Olga, was the youngest daughter of the Wegner family.

The next day, Olga peeked her head in the doorway of the harness shop and threw a crabapple at Judge. It hit him square in the forehead. She then teasingly said, "Hi George!" And so, the romance began.[1] Olga must have been one of those "good fish in the sea that have never been caught" Judge wrote about in his January 18, 1919 letter from Germany when he realized Ruby's letters had stopped.

One unforgettable day while working in the harness shop, Judge heard a blood-curdling scream coming from the meat market. He rushed next door to find Olga had accidently caught her hand in a meat grinder. She had been feeding meat into the grinder when it pulled in her hand. Four of her fingers had been mangled. Judge rushed her to Willmar on the train to find a doctor.[2]

The local newspaper stated "only quick thinking in turning off the machine saved her from far greater injury."[3]

Olga's disfigured hand healed, but only a thumb remained on her left hand. She developed a fear of doctors after the traumatic incident. She was never photographed with her left hand visible after that day. Some of the town women asked Judge if he wanted a cripple for a wife. Olga herself asked Judge if he still wanted a woman with missing fingers. Judge replied that it made no difference to him whether she had fingers or not.[4]

The only source of controversy surrounding their marriage was that Olga was a Lutheran, and Judge was a Methodist, a "mixed" marriage by Raymond's standards. Olga's Lutheran pastor Rev. J. Seitzinger, conducted the wedding ceremony in 1923 with Judge's younger brother Roy serving as best man. But after they were married, Olga surprisingly left her German Lutheran church and "defected" to the maverick Methodists. Some Lutherans in Raymond held a grudge against them for quite some time.[5]

At the time of their wedding, Judge was 27 years old. Olga was 19. In their wedding photo, Olga wore her wedding ring on her right hand; her left hand was discreetly hidden beneath pink roses on her lap.

Olga had an older brother who served in World War I. Pvt. 1st Class William J. Wegner, Jr. served in France with Company C,

Fifth Engineers, Seventh Division, a division that saw very little front line action.

She also had an uncle who fought in the war. But, he did not serve with the Americans, he fought for the Germans. Richard Kropp, a brother of Olga's mother who did not immigrate, fought and died in the Battle of Tannenberg on the Eastern front, one month after the war began in 1914. Despite the battle being a huge German victory over the Russians, Richard became an early casualty of the war somewhere near Tannenberg.[6]

On January 8, 1915, well before the US entered the war, the *Raymond News* wrote, "Reports came here that Richard Kropp a soldier in the German army was killed in a battle a few weeks ago. Mr. Kropp is a brother to L. J. Kropp and Mrs. W. J. Wagner of this place."

In a deserted cemetery in Europe, a memorial stone sits in memory of Olga's uncle. The cemetery, once in Gembitz-Hauland, Germany, is now part of western Poland, just east of Czarnkow. The cemetery contains only a few remaining legible headstones. One of them reads, "In quiet memory to our father and husband who died in the World War. Richard Kropp, born 29 December 1876, died in battle 28 August 1914 in Tannenberg where he lies."

It also reads, "Greater love has no one than this; to lay down one's life for one's friends" -John 15:13.[7]

Not surprisingly, anti-German sentiment was prevalent in the US during and after the war years, and the small village of Raymond, Minnesota was no exception despite its sizable presence of prominent German immigrants including both Olga's parents. Her father Wilhelm Wagner was a charter member of St. John's Lutheran Church in town, which was originally called the German Lutheran Church. Prior to the war, church services were held exclusively in German. Its first resident pastor Rev. E. Beyer was born in Germany. In Olga's early years at the church, Raymond-born children learned High German and were confirmed in German.

The war changed things. Many churches in the US dropped their German sermons as a way to deemphasize their ties to the fatherland. In Raymond, the German Lutherans introduced their first English sermon delivered by Rev. Rudolph Lechner just after the war ended. According to St. John's 100th anniversary booklet however, the use of the German language did not entirely end until after World War II in 1950 when Rev. Lechner gave his last sermon in German. By that time, many of the immigrant pioneers had passed away. English was used exclusively after 61 years of German services and 32 years of German/English services.

The Raymond News reported on boycotts of German products. One interesting headline of December 6, 1918 read, "GERMAN TRICKERY," adding:

A little incident showing Germany's unscrupulousness in trade was told the other day by the manager of a Chicago typewriter concern. "Before the War," he said, "the label 'Made in Germany' was known around the world. But it did not always tell the truth. Typewriters, cash registers, adding machines and other articles in the manufacture of which Americans excel, were shipped in large consignments to Hamburg.

"When they reached their destinations, sometimes two or three thousand miles from Hamburg, they bore the 'Made in Germany' label. America, of course, received the money, but Germany got some very good free advertising. We will have to look out for the Boches when the war is over.

Judge had no qualms concerning Olga's Germanic nature. But did it have any bearing on their decision as a wedded couple to walk past Olga's Lutheran church every Sunday and attend the Methodist church two blocks away? Perhaps. However, the main reason they left the German Lutheran church was because the Lutherans frowned on the Methodist Judge. It was not a case of Judge preferring a non-German church, it was the German Lutherans who had difficulty accepting a "lowly" Methodist sitting in their pews.

Finally, it was Olga who said "enough" and decided they would worship at the Methodist church. Many of the Lutherans never forgave them.

Where Judge and Olga attended church was a choice of major importance, and they were well aware of the imminent scrutiny and consequential flak they would receive from relatives and neighbors for "snubbing" the German Lutherans. Church denominations were a big deal in Raymond, and it went beyond Sunday mornings. Despite all this, Olga wouldn't tolerate anyone looking down on her husband for being a Methodist. No way. So, she became one, too, along with her children.

At Christmastime in 1926, Judge was sent a Ninetieth Division bulletin of Christmas greetings. In it was a letter from the Ninetieth Division's commander General Henry T. Allen.

"What an inspiration it was and remains, to have seen that superb 90th Division at grips with a most redoubtable enemy, oblivious apparently to the fact that death was stalking their advance step by step . . . Good soldiers and good citizens are almost synonymous terms and I can assure you that you are worthily and patriotically fulfilling your duties as citizens by your fine service to the flag," he wrote. "It is indeed a great pleasure to send you Christmas Greetings from the Capitol of our country which you so nobly honored."

Over the next several years, Judge and Olga had four children: Robert, Mildred, Dorothy, and Elaine. During the Great Depression, the family always had enough to eat, especially meat since Olga's family owned the meat market. They happily ate plenty of bologna. They also raised chickens and a cow named "Minnie."

Still a man of compassion, Judge did what he could to help people in Raymond during the toughest of economic times. He and Olga maintained a half-acre vegetable garden that supplied food for the family, and many of the older citizens in town.

Hobos slept all over Raymond and in the prairies during the Depression, and Judge put some to work with odd jobs such as sharpening scissors and knives, or fetching water from the well. The trees in front of Judge's house were marked with chalk by the hobos. The hobos had a system of communicating with each other through various symbols meaning such things as "good place for a handout" or "kind gentlemen lives here" or "vicious dog here."

Sometimes a coat was provided for warmth, other times it was a meal. While Judge was no longer a child sneaking eggs, he still sought to help. It was just in his nature. He also knew what it was like to be discouraged, cold, wet, hungry, thirsty, and filthy. Some of the hobos were most-likely fellow veterans of the war. "Mom and Dad never turned anyone away," Mildred said.

As a young girl, Mildred ate meals with the hobos, just as Judge once did as a boy. Her grandmother Wegner told her never to think less of the men as they were "good people who were just down on their luck." Mildred remembered one man in particular who came into Raymond the same time each fall. One autumn, she looked for him. When she finally glimpsed him down the road, she ran to him and held his hand. Together they walked to the Knott home. Years later, that same man surprisingly appeared at Judge's harness shop to tell him Judge's young daughter saved his life with her trust in him after he became a homeless, unemployed alcoholic during the Depression.

Mildred remembered her dad liked to fish and hunt, additional ways to augment the family food supply. During hunting expeditions in the cornfields of Raymond, her job was to "chase up the pheasants. Dad never missed a shot," she said.

In 1931, Judge received sad news that his Minnesota friend from Company G, Richard F. Peters, had died of a stroke at age 36 at Veterans Hospital in Minneapolis, Minnesota. Richard and Judge had spent nearly their entire wartime together, first meeting at Camp Travis.

They were fellow Minnesotans who fought with the Texas boys, and developed the rare bond experienced by brothers in arms. While Judge felt sad he could not afford to attend any Ninetieth

Division reunions since the war, he did keep in contact with Richard and stayed close until Richard's death. Mildred said she remembered he visited the family in Raymond once. Judge learned of his death in a letter from Richard's mother.

> *Dear Friend:*
> *Allow me to call you friend since I know you were a very dear friend of Richard's. I am enclosing a clipping from our paper telling you of Richard's death on May 31st. . . Richard spoke of you and his pals in the army and I know he thought a great deal of you.*
> *Your friend,*
> *Mrs. Peters*

All too soon, Judge had to live through another world war. But this time, it was not his turn to fight; that obligation fell to his son, Robert. Judge watched his only son leave to fight in World War II. Judge was no longer the young soldier--he was the parent of a young soldier and was forced to confront an entirely different perspective of war.

One of Judge's daughters, Dorothy Knott Rude, recalled the anxiety of her parents at that time.[8] "I remember December 7, 1941 when the Japanese bombed Pearl Harbor. We had come home from church, had dinner, and were clearing the dishes when the announcement came on the radio. My parents were very worried because they knew brother Bob would be going into service along with all the Wegner cousins," she said.

Robert Knott, however, safely returned home after serving with the US Navy in the Pacific.

Judge and Olga spent a long, peaceful life in Raymond. Seemingly content with his one great adventure in life, Judge had no desire to travel. He loved the comfort and security of home.

Once, and only once, Judge went out drinking with his American Legion buddies after a meeting around 1940. Their destination was Clara City. Clara City, just seven miles away, was considered a den of iniquity to some in Raymond. Clara City was in a neighboring "wet" county. Raymond was located in Kandiyohi County, which was still "dry" and would remain so until 1965. It was one of the last counties in Minnesota to allow liquor sales.

Apparently, the 3.2 strength beer sold in Raymond wasn't going to satisfy the Legion men that night. Of course, this got Judge in trouble with Olga, who strongly disapproved of alcohol. Going to Clara City meant something to the people of Raymond, and it wasn't good. Even Judge's daughters weren't supposed to date the "wild boys from Clara City."[9]

During baseball season, everyone in town knew not to pay a call when the Minnesota Twins or Boston Red Sox played as Judge and Olga were glued to the radio or television. They also loved to play Whist and Buck Euchre, popular card games of the time. Judge took up tennis, often playing doubles with a local doctor named C. C. Walker. Not surprisingly, Judge and Olga were active in the United Methodist Church (it had dropped the Episcopal part of its name), school and community activities. Judge served as trustee on the Raymond Village Council.

Judge raised a variety of terriers over the years, although none rose to the level of esteem enjoyed by Duke.

Judge, along with brothers Ten and Bill, were charter members of the Peter Leuze American Legion Post #420, which was founded in 1920. It was one of a million posts that sprang up across the country soon after the Great War's veterans returned home.[10]

Two years after he came home, Ten married Isabel Ryder, the young lady who frequently wrote the Knott boys during the war, and raised six children on a farm in Raymond.

Bill was the last of the Knott doughboys to marry in 1929. He and wife Ida had three children. He never made it out west, but instead lived and worked as a carpenter in Illinois. Eventually, Bill returned with his family to reside in Raymond.

Bill's youngest daughter Ginny Knott Ogibovic described the village of Raymond of her childhood as something resembling a Norman Rockwell painting. During the late 1940s through 1960s, she said the only vacant building in town was her grandfather's old cream shop. Judge's harness shop was something of a Raymond institution for the men.

"South of the cream shop was my Uncle George's harness shop where he repaired harnesses and sold feed for the livestock. He also sold Red Wing Shoes for anyone willing to brush the dust off the boxes," Ginny wrote in an August 21, 2013 letter to *The Raymond News*.

"The shop was a haven for the men, and according to my mom, they liked gathering there because there was no phone in the building so their wives couldn't contact them . . . The group that was huddled around the oil burner were usually in a hot political discussion.

"Every Saturday night families came to town for their weekly shopping. The ladies shopped while the men either sat in their car to wait or gathering in Uncle George's harness shop for good conversation," she added.

In 1963, Judge and Olga celebrated their fortieth wedding anniversary. Their marriage proved a good match; their strengths and personalities complimented each another's. The name Ruby, however, was never mentioned in Olga's presence.

Judge and Olga's anniversary garnered a prominent write up in the local newspaper, *The Raymond News.*[11] The news story interestingly lists many relatives in attendance at the celebration, then singles out one notable exception:

Only one member of the family, Dennis Zetah, could not be present for the occasion as he was serving in the army reserve at Camp McCoy, Wis, at that time.

Poor Dennis!

In addition to the *Raymond News*, Judge read three newspapers every day: *The Minneapolis Star, St. Paul Pioneer,* and *Willmar*

Tribune. He also liked pulp westerns, which he shared with Ten, Bill, and Roy.

Judge sold his harness shop at 208 Cofield Street in 1963 and retired. He had dropped the harness repair since there weren't many horses left in Raymond. He ended up mostly selling and repairing shoes at the end, mainly Red Wing Shoes. Red Wing Shoes, a Minnesota company, had primarily supplied the doughboys with boots during the war. The harness shop building now houses the Raymond Public Library.

Memorial Day was a special day in Raymond. Judge carried a gun and marched with the Legion in the parade. Olga carried the US flag for the Auxiliary. "He loved to march and was so proud they marched for General Pershing. He looked forward to Memorial Day and the thrill of marching again," Mildred said.

Judge's children said they felt lucky to have such a loving father and idyllic childhood growing up in Raymond.[12]

"My dad was very special – always loving, smiling and giving kisses," said Dorothy. "Every Sunday afternoon all the Knott relatives met at Grandpa Knott's home. The Knott cousins always had a good time playing together. Every Fourth of July was spent at the Tennus Knott farm for a huge Knott family picnic and after dark Ben Mielker, friend of the family, would shoot off skyrockets and Roman candle fireworks . . . there was always a lot of laughter and fun going on."

Mildred added, "I was always so proud of my dad. He never lost his strong faith and sense of humor. I wrote a song about my daddy and sang it at a Knott reunion. I'll never forget his face. He told me that he was so proud."

My daddy is tall and lean
With red curly hair
He always was happy
He always was there
He looked at the sunshine

When the going got dim
Oh Lord I'm so lucky
To have a daddy like him

My Daddy by Mildred Knott Robbins

Mildred's lyrics were simple, but insightful. As a young man, Judge had witnessed the ugly realities of life. But, he had also experienced the beauty. Now an old man, Judge had been blessed with life's joy, laughter, and profound love. As he wrote from Germany in the winter of 1919:

It would never do for a soldier to have the homesickness blues all the time, or he would spoil the little good time he has.

Inevitably, the surviving doughboys began to die off. The Knotts were somewhat known for their longevity, but Judge's brother Bill was the first to go in 1955 at age 60. Judge's cousin Ray Knott died in Arizona in 1968, after living many years in Montana working as a clerk. Ten passed away in 1972.

Olga died due to heart complications in 1971. Judge and Olga had lived together for many decades in a Dutch colonial at 304 Agnes Street in Raymond.

After Olga's death, Judge liked to relax on his front porch and watch the world go by. Along with sports, he enjoyed watching game shows on his black and white television. His favorite shows included *Jeopardy!* and *Hollywood Squares,* with Charlie Weaver and Paul Lynde being the favorite squares. When Weaver or Lynde were featured, everyone in the room had to be quiet and listen.[13]

Judge walked everywhere he went in Raymond . . . to the post office, church, and bank, humming along the way. Always fond of telling funny and interesting stories, he often ended them with, "Isn't that a corker?"

Late in 1975, Judge was diagnosed with cancer. Donald Knott, Judge's nephew and Ten's son, along with Donald's wife LuAnn, recalled that Judge kept his trademark sense of humor to the end.[14]

"When I would drive him to the doctor in Willmar, he always had a joke," LuAnn said.

One visit, the doctor made an off-color remark. Judge and LuAnn wouldn't dare look at each in the doctor's office for fear of losing their composure and bursting out in laughter. But, once in the car, "We plain hee-hawed. We laughed so loud," she said. "He always had stories."

LuAnn also kindly drove Olga to the doctor in Clara City during her last months.

The night Judge died, LuAnn remembered getting the telephone call at about 3:00 a.m. "He passed away in the same bed as his wife," she said. Today, Donald and LuAnn Knott still live in Raymond, just across the street from Judge's childhood home.

Mildred spent time with her father at the end.[15] She said he "died with dignity. He was the most positive person I have ever seen facing death." Judge told her he loved being with her, but it was time to be with Olga. He never complained, often declining morphine for the pain. "He considered his next life to be something to look forward to," Mildred said.

Judge's pastor, Rev. Ronald Guderian, visited him the day before he died. "He was very calm, and I would say . . . very happy," Ronald said. "He welcomed it (death). I knew him well. He was a good friend."[16]

Pastor Guderian conducted Judge's funeral at the Methodist church in Raymond, where neighbor Calvin Dykema sang *How Great Thou Art* and *Under his Wings*:[17]

Under his wings, oh, what precious enjoyment!
There I will hide till life's trials are o'er;
Sheltered, protected, no evil can harm me,
Resting in Jesus I'm safe evermore.

Of all five Knott boys in the Great War, Pvt. George "Judge" R. Knott was the last doughboy to die on February 6, 1977. He was

80 years old. A Tough 'Ombre to the end. He is buried in Fairview Cemetery in Raymond, next to Olga, and near his brothers Ten and Bill. At the United Methodist Church, the Olga and George Knott Memorial Garden grows in their memory.

Judge Knott c. 1920; family photo.

Judge in his harness shop wearing his new "uniform"
Oshkosh B'gosh overalls c. 1921; family photo.

Judge and Olga, family photos.

Judge with son Robert, Ben Mielker, and Elaine during World War II; family photo.

1952 family photo (standing l-r) Dorothy,
Robert, Mildred; (seated l-r) Elaine, Judge, Olga.

Judge and Olga; family photo.

Judge's uniform and medals, family photos 2013;
the woolen uniform is incredibly course and scratchy.

Judge's leggings, medals, honorable discharge
lapel pin, American Legion hat; family photo 2013.

Acknowledgments

This book would never have been written without the guidance of Judge Knott's oldest daughter, Mildred Knott Robbins of Cedar Hill, Missouri. Millie had the foresight in the 1970s to formally interview her father, and record his experiences in the war. Many years later, for some reason, Millie presented me with Judge's war correspondence, uniform, and memorabilia — even though she had six children to pass them along to. Millie is a sentimental saver of family things. Thank you, Millie.

There are many more Knott relations I wish to acknowledge, many of Millie's generation, who helped supply the rich details and nuances I needed to capture. I felt if I didn't get this story right with their generation, I wasn't going to get it right, period. Special thanks to Dottie Knott Rude, of Menomonee Falls, Wisconsin; Dennis Zetah and Elaine "Kooz" Knott Zetah of Hutchinson, Minnesota; Donald and Lu Ann Knott of Raymond, Minnesota; Gerri Knott Ekblad of Yucaipa, California; Ginny Knott Ogibovic of La Porte, Indiana; Candice Knott Holloway of Flagstaff, Arizona; Loren Knott of Burnsville, Minnesota; and Gayel Knott of New Westminster, British Columbia, Canada.

The Kandiyohi County Historical Society, Minnesota Historical Society, Raymond News, and archivists at the National Personnel Records Center in St. Louis, Missouri were also invaluable resources; along with the many digitized volumes of US Army and archival sources and websites now online, many of which were not available just a few years ago. These websites include the 90th Division Association (of which I am a proud honorary member), and the genealogical wiki site werelate.org, which enabled me to find shirttail Knott cousins I did not know existed.

Thanks to historian, friend, and co-worker, the über-capable Katy Zignego of Oconomowoc, Wisconsin, interlibrary-loan librarian extraordinaire, who magically found and supplied me with rare books and obscure microfilm from all parts of the country. Katy urged me to write this book and dispensed plenty of high fives along the way, as only we library nerds can do.

Of course, I wish to thank my husband Jon and sons Alex and Kyle, who suffered through me half listening to them for months on end as my mind was in another century, and who put up with stacks of papers and books piled throughout our home. They also answered my seemingly-endless requests for help and advice.

I also thank Adolph Caso and Branden Books of Boston, who took a chance on a first-time book author.

Lastly, I acknowledge the Lord, who lit my path and did the same for my grandfather, Judge Knott. I am grateful to be able to tell his story.

Jennifer Rude Klett
October 2013

Notes

Chapter 2: The Knott Boys
1. Family stories: Gerri Knott Ekblad, *The Knott Family History* (1995) 23-25. Gerri is Bill Knott's daughter.
2. Family history: Mildred Knott Robbins letter December 2005. Mildred is Judge Knott's daughter who formally interviewed and recorded Judge's memories of the war.
3. Family stories: Knott Ekblad, *The Knott Family History*, 24.
4. Henry G. Young, president Kandiyohi War Records Committee, *Kandiyohi County in the World War 1917-1918-1919,* (Kandiyohi War Records Committee, 1928) 81.
5. Family history: Knott Ekblad, *The Knott Family History*, 10.
6. The Medical Department of the United States Army in the World War, Volume XV Statistics, (Part One Army Anthropology, 1921), 36.
7. Colonel Leonard P. Ayres, The War With Germany: a Statistical Summary, (US Government Printing Office, 1919) Chapter 1, Map 1.
8. The Medical Department of the United States Army in the World War, (Part One Army Anthropology, 1921) 34. Accessed ebook online April 23, 2013. This source lists copious amounts of measurement charts from World War I recruits with comparisons to Civil War soldiers and racial comparisons.

Chapter 3: The Alamo's "Hell Fire and a Fuzzy-O"
1. Colonel Leonard Pl Ayres, The War With German: A Statistical Summary, (US Government Printing Office, 1919) Chapter 1, Diagram 7.
2. Ibid, Chapter 1, Map 1.
3. The Medical Department of the United States Army in the World War, (Part One Army Anthropology, 1921) 35.
4. Major George Wythe, *A History of the 90th Division* (90th Division Association, 1920), 3.

5. 360th Infantry National Army, *A Short History and Photographic Record of the 360th Infantry Texas Brigade* (1918), 3.
6. Ibid, 3.
7. Lonnie J. White, *The 90th Division In World War I*, (Sunflower University Press, 1996) 59.
8. Ibid, 161-163.
9. Ibid, 32.
10. War Service Record, request # 2-11504826230, National Archives National Personnel Records Center, St. Louis, MO.
11. Wythe, *A History of the 90th Division*, 8.
12. White, *The 90th Division In World War I*, 53.
13. Lonnie J. White, "CAMP TRAVIS," Handbook of Texas Online
(http://www.tshaonline.org/handbook/online/articles/qbc28),
accessed March 25, 2013. Published by the Texas State Historical Association.
14. Ibid.

Chapter 4: Over There
1. Colonel Leonard P. Ayres, The War With Germany: a Statistical Summary, (US Government Printing Office, 1919) Figures Of American Participation In The War
(http://net.lib.byu.edu/estu/wwi/memoir/docs/statistics/statstc.htm#4) accessed April 22, 2013.
2. PBS, *The Great War And the Shaping of the 20th Century*, PBS online,
(http://www.pbs.org/greatwar/resources/casdeath_pop.html)
accessed February, 2013. This series is currently not available on DVD, only VHS.
3. Lonnie J. White, *The 90th Division In World War I*, 78-79.
4. Wythe, *A History of the 90th Division*, 16.
5. Ibid, 26.
6. Ibid, 25.
7. Ibid, 25.

Chapter 5: Over the Top at St. Mihiel
1. Wythe, *A History of the 90th Division*, 32, 77.
2. Lonnie J. White, *The 90th Division In World War I*, 87.
3. Ibid, xvi, 35.
4. Ibid, 23.
5. Ibid, 51.
6. The Institute of Heraldry>Categories>Regiments>360th Regiment, Office of the Administrative Assistant to the Secretary of the Army, (http://www.tioh.hqda.pentagon.mil/Heraldry/ArmyDUISSICOA/ ArmyHeraldryUnit.aspx?u=4174), accessed April 13, 2013. The Insignia and Coat of Arms was redesigned in 1962.
7. Family history: Mildred Knott Robbins letter, December 2005. The terms foxhole and funk hole were both used to describe a hole dug for protection. Foxhole became the more popular term after World War I ended.

Chapter 6: "I Am Trying My Best To Shoot Them"
1. Wythe, *A History of the 90th Division*, 63.
2. Ibid, 66.
3. Ibid, 67.

Chapter 7: The Battle of Meuse-Argonne
1. United States Department of Health and Human Services website, *The Great Pandemic: the United States in 1918-1919* (http://www.flu.gov/pandemic/history/1918/the_pandemic/legacyp endemic/index.html), accessed March 26, 1013.
2. Major George Wythe, *A History of the 90th Division* (90th Division Association, 1920), 94-96.
3. Ibid, 96-98.
4. Ibid, 98.
5. Ibid, 99.
6. a. Ibid.

6. b. Lonnie J White, The 90th Division In World War I, 136.
7. Army of Occupation AEF, *A History Of The Activities And Operations Of The 360th United States Infantry Regiment In The World War, 1914-1918*, 32.
8. Wythe, *A History Of The 90th Division*, 99.
9. Ibid, 105.
10. Army of Occupation AEF, *A History Of The Activities And Operations Of The 360th United States Infantry Regiment In The World War, 1914-1918*, 30, 36.
11. Lonnie J. White, *The 90th Division In World War I*, 129-130.
12. Dennis Zetah, telephone interview, 2013.
13. Joseph Persico, *Eleventh Month, Eleventh Day, Eleventh Hour Armistice Day, 1918, World War I and Its Violent Climax*, (Random House, 2004), 378.
14. Gerri Knott Ekblad, *The Knott Family History* (1995), 23. Outhouse tipping was the thing to do in Raymond. Judge and his brother Roy once tried to tip over John Wagner's outhouse, but found he was inside using it. John Wagner, Judge's girlfriend Ruby's dad, began yelling so they waited at a distance until he was done. Then, they finished the job. Judge and Roy later had to right the outhouse and apologize.

Chapter 8: Alamo Division Numbers and Notables
1. Wythe, *A History of the 90th Division*, (90th Division Association, 1920), xv
2. Ibid, xvi.
3. Army of Occupation AEF, *A History Of The Activities And Operations Of The 360th United States Infantry Regiment In The World War*, 1914-1918, 61.
4. Wythe, *A History of the 90th Division*, 154.

Chapter 9: Post Armistice and the March to Germany

1. Army of Occupation AEF, *A History Of The Activities And Operations Of The 360th United States Infantry Regiment In The World War, 1914-1918*, 48.
2. Wythe, *A History of the 90th Division*, (90th Division Association, 1920), 186.
3. Gerri Knott Ekblad, letter to the author, 2006; Loren R. Knott, in-person interview, 2013.
4. Encyclopedia of Genealogy website (http://www.eogen.com/USWorldWarIDraftRegistrations) accessed August 2013.
5. Gerri Knott Ekblad, letter to the author, 2006; Loren R. Knott, in-person interview, 2013.

Chapter 10: Living With the Germans
1. Family history: Mildred Knott Robbins letter December 2005.
2. Wythe, *A History of the 90th Division*, (90th Division Association, 1920), 193-195.
3. War Service Record, request # 2-11504826230, National Archives National Personnel Records Center, St. Louis, MO.

Chapter 11: Home
1. National Archives website (http://www.archives.gov/global-pages/larger-image.html?i=/historical-docs/doc-content/images/mothers-day-proc-l.jpg&c=/historical-docs/doc-content/images/mothers-day-proc.caption.html), accessed April 15, 2013.
2. Family history: Mildred Knott Robbins letter December 2005.
3. Department of the Navy-Naval History and Heritage Command website (http://www.history.navy.mil/photos/sh-civil/civsh-m/mongolia.htm), accessed April 15, 2013.
4. Lonnie J. White, *The 90th Division In World War I*, 204.
5. Ibid, 207.
6. Family history: Mildred Knott Robbins letter December 2005.

7. Family history: Donald Knott telephone interview February 2013. Donald is Ten Knott's son.

8. Ibid.

9. Family history: Mildred Knott Robbins telephone interview February 2013.

10. Family history: Dennis Zetah telephone interview February 2013.

Chapter 12: Carlton Knott and the Lost Battalion

1. Burial Cast File request 2-11409034948, National Archives National Personnel Records Center, St. Louis, MO.

2. 77th Division Association, designed and written in the field-France, *History of the seventy seventh Division, August 25, 1917, November 11th, 1918* (W.H. Crawford Company, 1919) 206.

3. Robert H. Ferrell, *Five Days In October: The Lost Battalion Of World War I* (University of Missouri Press, 2005) *vii.*

4. a. L. Wardlaw Miles, *History of the 308th Infantry* (http://www.longwood.k12.ny.us/history/upton/miles/miles.htm) Chapter 6, page 3.

4 b. War Service Record, request #2-11403271677, National Archives National Personnel Records Center, St. Louis, MO.

5. L. Wardlaw Miles, *History of the 308th Infantry* (http://www.longwood.k12.ny.us/history/upton/miles/miles.htm) Chapter 6, page 3.

6. War Department, Army War College, *The Operation of the So-Called 'Lost Battalion'* (National Archives at Washington, DC, Textual Records Series: Historical Files, compiled 1918-1948, 1928) 1.

7. Reprinted from pages 30-31 of *Five Days In October: The Lost Battalion Of World War I* by Robert H. Ferrell, by permission of the University of Missouri-Press. Copyright © 2005 by the Curators of the University of Missouri.

8. 77th Division Association, designed and written in the field-France, *History of the seventy seventh Division, August 25, 1917, November 11th, 1918* (W.H. Crawford Company, 1919) 206.

9. Reprinted from pages 78-79 of *Five Days In October: The Lost Battalion Of World War I* by Robert H. Ferrell, by permission of the University of Missouri-Press. Copyright © 2005 by the Curators of the University of Missouri.

10. American Legion website (http://www.legion.org/troops/bluestar) accessed July 20, 2013; American Gold Star Mothers, Inc. website (http://www.goldstarmoms.com/WhoWeAre/History/History.htm) accessed July 20, 2013. No records of Bertha Knott Phiefer were found after searching the archived files of American Gold Star Mothers, Inc., 9 August 2013.

11. Burial Case File request 2-11409034948, National Archives National Personnel Records Center, St. Louis, MO, 2013. Carlton's emergency address lists Mrs. Daisy Helen McCallum, 323 Wallace Ave, Coeur d'Elene, Idaho. The relationship between Carlton and this woman is unknown. Carlton listed the same address in 1918, so they may have been fellow boarders of a Wallace Ave. residence.

12. Thomas M. Johnson and Fletcher Pratt, *The Lost Battalion* (University of Nebraska Press, 2000, original publication 1938), 314.

13. Burial Case File request 2-11409034948, National Archives National Personnel Records Center, St. Louis, MO.

14. Family history: Ray Knott letter supplied by his granddaughter Candice Knott Holloway, email interview May 2013.

15. Robert H. Ferrell, *Five Days In October*, 83.

16. Ibid, 86.

17. Burial Case File, National Archives National Personnel Records Center, St. Louis, MO.

18. Ibid.

19. Ibid.

20. Family history: Judge Knott's children only vaguely remembered a Carlton Knott and had no idea of the circumstances of his death. Ray Knott's granddaughter Candice Knott Holloway of Arizona inherited Ray's letter about visiting Carlton's grave in France. No Knott source contacted seems to know anything about Carlton's wife or child. No record of a marriage or divorce or birth of a baby has been found, particularly by the county clerk and clerk of court in Cascade County, Montana, and the Montana Historical Society.

Chapter 13: A Tough 'Ombre To The End
1. Family history: Mildred Knott Robbins telephone interview February 2013.
2. Ibid.
3. Newspaper article, Mildred Knott Robbins. This clipping is not attributed to any newspaper; it is most likely from the *Raymond News* or *Willmar Tribune*.
4. Family history: Mildred Knott Robbins, telephone interview February 2013.
5. Family history: Dorothy Knott Rude, interview 2005.
6. *The Raymond News*, January 8, 1915.
7. Family history: Family History of Wilhelmine Drager Wegner Harmel 1833-1902, Mary C. Curtis, 1994, 29.
8. Family history: Dorothy Knott Rude, memoirs December 7, 2001.
9. Family history: Dorothy Knott Rude, interview 2005.
10. The American Legion website
(http://www.legion.org/history) accessed April 15, 2013.
11. *The Raymond News*, August 30, 1963.
12. Family history: Dorothy Knott Rude, memoirs December 7, 2001.
13. Family history: Jennifer Rude Klett, memoirs 2005.
14. Family history: LuAnn Knott, letter October 6, 2006; telephone interview February 2013.

15. Family history: Mildred Knott Robbins, letter December 2005.
16. Family history: Rev. Ronald Guderian, telephone interview April 2013.
17. Hymn: William Orcutt Cushing, *Under His Wings*, 1896.
    Obituary: *The Raymond News*, March 24, 1977.

Bibliography:

American Armies and Battlefields in Europe. American Battle Monuments Commission, Washington, D.C.: United States Government Printing Office, 1938.

Wythe, Major George. *History of the 90th Division*. 90th Division Association, 1920.

A Short History and Photographic Record of the 360th Infantry Texas Brigade. Texas: San Antonio Printing Co., 1918.

"Ninetieth Division Bulletin Xmas Greetings". San Antonio, Texas, December 25, 1926.

Ekblad, Gerri Knott. *The Knott Family History, 1800s and 1900s*. Yucaipa, California, 1995.

Ferrell, Robert H.,ed. *Five Days In October: The Lost Battalion of World War I*. Columbia, Missouri: University of Missouri Press, 2005.

Raymond, Minnesota 100 Years: Working, Worshipping, Living, Learning Together. Raymond, Minnesota: The Raymond News Raymond Centennial Book Committee, 1988.

Kandiyohi County In The World War 1917-1918-1919. Kandiyohi War Records Committee, Willmar, Minnesota, 1928.

Hallas, James H. *Doughboy War: The American Expeditionary Force in World War I*. London: Lynne Rienner Publishers, Inc., 2000.

Mead, Gary. *The Doughboys: American and the First World War.* Woodstock and New York: Overlook Press, 2000.

One Hundredth Anniversary St. John's Lutheran Church. Raymond, Minnesota: St. John's Lutheran Church, 1989.

Freidel, Frank. *Over There: The Story of America's First Great Overseas Crusade.* Philadelphia: Temple University Press, 1990.

Persico, Joseph E. *Eleventh Month, Eleventh Day, Eleventh Hour, Armistice Day, 1918, World War I and Its Violent Climax.* New York: Random House, 2004.

Stallings, Laurence. *The Doughboys: The Story of the AEF, 1917-1918.* New York: Harper and Row, 1963.

Freidel, Frank. *Over There, the American Experience In World War I.* New York: Bramhall House, 1964.

The Methodist Sunday School Hymnal. Cincinnati: Jennings & Graham, New York: Eaton & Mains, Board of Sunday Schools of the Methodist Episcopal Church, John R. Van Pelt, Peter C. Lutkin, 1911.

Johnson, Thomas and Fletcher Pratt. *The Lost Battalion.* Lincoln, Nebraska: University of Nebraska Press, 2000.

United Methodist Church Raymond, Minnesota. Raymond, Minnesota: United Methodist Church, 1980.

National Personnel Records Center, 9700 Page Avenue, St. Louis, MO 63132.

Rubin, Richard. *The Last Of The Doughboys: The Forgotten*

Generation And Their Forgotten World War, New York: Houghton Mifflin Harcourt Publishing Company, 2013.

White, Lonnie J. "CAMP TRAVIS," *Handbook of Texas Online* (http://www.tshaonline.org/handbook/online/articles/qbc28), accessed March 25, 2013, published by the Texas State Historical Association.

White, Lonnie J. *The 90th Division In World War I*. Sunflower University Press, 1996.

The Institute of Heraldry website >Categories> Regiments>360th Regiment, Office of the Administrative Assistant to the Secretary of the Army, (http://www .tioh.hqda.pentagon.mil/Heraldry/Army DUISSICOA/ArmyHeraldryUnit.aspx?u=4174).

United States Department of Health and Human Services website, *The Great Pandemic: the United States in 1918-1919* (http://www.flu.gov/pandemic/history/1918/the_pandemic/legacyp endemic/index.html).

Raymond High School Alumni 1911 to 1976. Raymond, Minnesota: 1976.

Ayres, Colonel Leonard P., *The War With Germany: A Statistical Summary*, second edition, US Government Printing Office, 1919.

Barnett, Victor F., Second Lieutenant, Headquarters Co., 360th Infantry, Army of Occupation, American Expeditionary Forces. *A History Of The Activities And Operations Of The 360th United States Infantry Regiment In The World War 1914-1918*, 1919.

Albertine, Connell. *The Yankee Doughboy*. Boston: Branden Press, 1968.

Index

Made in the USA
Charleston, SC
14 May 2014